THE BARCLAYS GUIDE TO
Financial Management
for the Small Business

Barclays Small Business Series

Series Editors: Colin Gray and John Stanworth

This new series of highly practical books aimed at new and established small businesses has been specially written by carefully selected authors in conjunction with the Small Business Unit of Barclays Bank. All the authors have a wide experience of the theory and, more important, the *practice* of small business and they address the problems that are likely to be encountered by new businesses in a clear and accessible way, including examples and case studies drawn from real business situations.

These comprehensive but compact guides will help owners and managers of small businesses to acquire the skills that are essential if they are to operate successfully in times of rapid change in the business environment.

The Barclays Guide to Marketing for the Small Business
Len Rogers

The Barclays Guide to Computing for the Small Business
Khalid Aziz

The Barclays Guide to International Trade for the Small Business
John Wilson

The Barclays Guide to Financial Management for the Small Business
Peter Wilson

The Barclays Guide to Managing Staff for the Small Business
Iain Maitland

The Barclays Guide to Growing the Small Business
Colin Gray

The Barclays Guide to Franchising for the Small Business
John Stanworth and Brian Smith

The Barclays Guide to Law for the Small Business
Stephen Lloyd

The Barclays Guide to Buying and Selling for the Small Business
John Gammon

THE BARCLAYS GUIDE TO
Financial
Management
for the Small Business

PETER WILSON

BARCLAYS
Published by
BLACKWELL

First published 1990

Basil Blackwell Ltd
108 Cowley Road, Oxford, OX4 1JF, UK

Basil Blackwell, Inc.
3 Cambridge Center
Cambridge, Massachusetts 02142, USA

British Library Cataloguing in Publication Data
A CIP catalogue record for this book is available from
the British Library

Library of Congress Cataloging in Publication Data
Wilson, Peter.
The Barclays guide to financial management for the small business
/ Peter Wilson.
p. cm.—(Barclays small business series)
ISBN 0–631–17253–X   ISBN 0–631–17254–8 (pbk.)
1. Small business—Finance.   I. Title.   II. Series.
HG4027.7.W55   1990
658.15'92—dc20   89–18552   CIP

Typeset in 10½ on 12½pt Plantin
by Hope Services (Abingdon) Ltd
Printed in Great Britain by
T. J. Press Ltd, Padstow, Cornwall

Contents

Contents

Foreword

The last five years have seen a significant growth in the number of small businesses in all sectors of industry in the UK. Unfortunately they have also seen an increase in the numbers of problems encountered by those businesses. Often the problems could have been avoided with the right help and advice.

Barclays, in association with Basil Blackwell, is producing this series of guides to give that help and advice. They are comprehensive and written in a straightforward way. Each one has been written by a specialist in the field, in conjunction with Barclays Bank, and drawing on our joint expertise to ensure that the advice given is appropriate.

With the aid of these guides the businessman or woman will be better prepared to face the many challenges ahead, and, hopefully, will be better rewarded for their efforts.

George Cracknell
Director UK Business
Sector Services
Barclays Bank plc

Preface

As the owner of a small business, you rarely have much time for financial matters, preferring to leave the accounting and information functions firmly in the lap of your accountants and information specialists. In terms of priorities, this attitude cannot be faulted, since without customers to buy and people to make and sell there would be no need for an understanding of finance at all. At some point, however, these priorities change and the more complex the business becomes, the greater is the need for an awareness of the role of financial management.

This short book seeks to redress an imbalance of financial skills in your small business. It is written from the standpoint of the non-accountant and non-financial manager. You probably do not have a financial qualification, yet you must display a talent for understanding the most detailed of financial reports and their implications and design financial reporting systems to suit the most complex of situations.

I believe that the sequence adopted in this book is the right one for the non-financial small business owner. It tackles finance and accounting with one object in view: to produce the right information for making decisions that will lead to the highest possible level of profit (or level of satisfaction). I trust that you will find the sequence logical and easy to follow.

My understanding of the financial needs of small firms has developed as a result of my work at The Enterprise Partnership, where we have been running small business management courses since 1983, and before that on the faculty at the London Business School. Some of these courses have broken new ground in the way that small business owners learn to think and to develop an awareness of their strategic task.

I am grateful to my partner, Phil Dowell, whose insights into small business development have helped to shape my thoughts in this book. Thanks are also due to Robert Lipman of Gordon Berman Chartered Accountants for some helpful advice on technical matters.

I

Financial management: why is it important?

Outline

This chapter introduces you to financial management. It will help you to understand:

- the importance of achieving and sustaining financial stability
- the critical role of cash in your business
- the need to understand the principles of good financial management

There is hardly a moment in the life of a small business when it is not important to know how much cash is in the bank, or how much is owed by customers or to suppliers. Furthermore, even a mildly curious business owner will want to know how the business is performing against its plans and budgets. The owner's ability to generate this basic kind of information requires some understanding of the practice of financial management.

Even in simple cash businesses – such as trading from a market stall – the owner needs to know how much to spend on stock and equipment and will have to forecast sales revenues in order to do this. Whereas a market stall trader will not need to produce anything more sophisticated than a few figures on the back of an envelope, questions about *financial resources* and *financial stability* (how much money is in the bank and how easily can the business continue to pay its debts) require constant attention, and decisions about what to spend money on, how much to spend and when to spend it cannot be made without the right *information*.

At a more personal level, the small business owner has to decide what the business can afford to pay him or her as a *salary* in recompense for long working hours, endless periods of worry, being innovative and putting personal capital at risk. In other words, the owner's return must be built into the financial equation.

The practice of financial management is much less concerned with accuracy than with *making profit* and *reducing risk*. Since the higher is the risk, the higher is the level of anxiety, there is no need to demonstrate that reducing risk is a desirable activity. Risk and uncertainty are closely related: the most risky situations are those where we have very little or no information and therefore where the greatest uncertainty exists. If there is uncertainty, there can be no effective control, and without control there is no way of knowing what the outcomes might be.

In the euphoria that surrounds the early years of setting up and establishing a business, the owner can be forgiven for paying less than due attention to financial management, other than staying on the right side of the bank manager. Most people get started because they want to be independent or want to achieve something on their own. Long hours and selfless devotion to the customer's needs are sufficient impetus to get the business moving in the right direction. But as the business starts to develop and the initial problems are overcome, aggregate sales income becomes relatively less important than the drive to make profits and to improve the quality of life. In the beginning there is little time to plan ahead and even less to ensure that the business develops a sound financial base.

This base is our principal concern in this book. How can the smaller business maintain a secure presence in an uncertain, risky and essentially hostile marketplace? What business procedures and financial control systems should be in place to ensure that financial stability endures? These are some of the questions that we shall be answering in the next few chapters.

Defining financial stability

What is an appropriate way to measure financial stability and what parts of the business must be controlled in order to achieve stability? Financial stability requires that the business should be able to repay all its current *outstanding debts* from income after collecting money from its customers, continue to be able to repay *future debts* when they fall due on the basis of future income collected from customers, have adequate liquid funds available at any time for *planned investments* in fixed assets (equipment, machinery, vehicles and buildings), and have access to adequate surplus funds to meet *unplanned needs*, or be able to access such funds readily through borrowing or the sale of equity.

These four requirements should ideally be met simultaneously. That they represent an ideal state of affairs acknowledges the problems of managing a small growing business and the priorities that the owners attach to generating sales and servicing the needs of their customers. Let us examine each of the requirements in turn.

Repaying current debts out of current income

It is a matter of common sense that a business which can pay its running costs and short-term debts (trade creditors, value-added tax (VAT), Pay As You Earn (PAYE) and the overdraft out of income received or soon to be received from customers is in a healthy state. This is the ultimate test of liquidity and we shall return to its relevance in a later chapter.

Repaying future debts out of future income

If the business can rely on future streams of income to cover its future debts (as defined above), then it is in an even sounder financial position. But since future income is hard to predict, the business will be more secure if future income is likely to exceed debts by a small margin.

Meeting investment needs out of internal funds

If the business can finance purchases of capital items out of internal funds (typically monies on short-term interest-bearing deposit accounts), it is financially sound. It may be unwise to commit all surplus funds to such longer-term investments and some borrowing may be a good idea to supplement internal funds, but this is a matter of judgement and financial strategy.

Meeting unplanned needs out of surplus funds

Business is about striking a balance between risk and reward and making decisions on the basis of sometimes inadequate information that affects this balance. Often these decisions are in response to unplanned threats or opportunities. Being in a comfortable position to meet such unplanned needs out of internal funds in addition to the above requirements, suggests that the business is as sound as it can ever be. Naturally, at times not all of these unplanned needs can be met internally and the business may have to borrow from its bank or, if circumstances warrant it, turn to the equity market for longer-term funds.

While the above four requirements for financial stability may appear to be unduly conservative, there can be no disputing them. The fundamental principle is that the business must be in a position to meet its debts and contingencies – both current and future – if it is to succeed in the longer term. Financial peace of mind need not be elusive if a few basic rules are followed. Nor does stability mean having large amounts of cash on deposit. Most businesses should be able to survive the bad times with a little belt tightening, a measure of financial common sense and the right monitoring and control systems.

Cash and profit: the basis of financial stability

The above four requirements suggest that the business needs *cash* to meet its current obligations. The best way to generate a sustained positive cash flow is to create *profit* from each and every transaction and ensure that financial controls turn profit into cash as quickly as possible. Thus while profit is a necessary condition for positive cash flow, it is by no means sufficient. There must be a reliable system for collecting payments from customers on time, while simultaneously paying bills due in an ordered way.

Furthermore, if the terms of trade can be negotiated so that cash arrives before it is spent, the reserves of cash held at the bank should cover the business adequately for any possible unplanned emergencies. Of course, many businesses are unable to organize their affairs quite so advantageously, but it is a mistake to assume that, because the rest of the industry operates in a certain way, the prevailing terms must necessarily be accepted without question. Although increasing competition gives the advantage to the buyer, everything is open to negotiation – the key is being able to make out a good case for being treated differently. We shall return to this point in a later chapter.

Businesses have been known to fail despite making a profit, because there has been no attempt to ensure that cash is released into the system at the proper time. The point is that *controls* are needed for positive cash flow. Thus we are concerned in this book with the management of both *cash* and *profit*: if positive outcomes can be secured for both, financial stability will follow automatically.

Understanding financial management

In order to be able to introduce the right kind of monitoring procedures and control systems, the owner wants to be in a position to understand the importance of financial accounting (accounting for the historical performance of the business) and management accounting (information requirements for current performance). There are three questions about the business that should be answered for effective financial management.

Question 1: How has the business performed in the past (and the reasons) and where does it stand at present?

It is entirely logical that, before planning ahead, it should be established exactly where the business is at present in terms of cash and profit and what has contributed to getting the business to its present position. The *profit and loss accounts, balance sheets* and *sources and applications of funds statements* over the last few years will need to be analysed. Answers to certain questions about past performance are required before looking into the future, not only because the owner needs to know why the business has performed as it has (which will allow the positive features to be developed while taking remedial action in the problem areas), but also because the future must in some way mirror the past. In other words, the relationships between sales and expenditure *in the past* will more or less determine *future* relationships. For example, if each £1 spent on advertising and promotional activities has generated £10 worth of sales in the past, it is unlikely that next year this relationship will change to any marked degree unless the business adopts an entirely new strategy. Moreover, the amount of finance (cash) required to generate each £1 of sales and net profit before tax *in the past* will more or less determine the amount required in the *future*.

Neither of these statements is supposed to suggest that financial relationships never change. Rather, they imply that there must be very good reasons for any proposed changes and that change should be *gradual* and *controlled*. Indeed, managing the rate of change effectively will determine the level of cash and profit generated over time. These issues are discussed in more depth in chapter 4.

Question 2: Where should the business go and how should it get there?

Most people run their businesses without really knowing where they are going. The activity known as *corporate planning* is simply a systematic way of setting out the *business objectives* (where the owner wants the business to go) for the coming period and the *strategy and plans* (how it will get there) to achieve these objectives. This is covered in depth in chapter 4, but at this point it is worth noting that, since the owner will need to produce forecasts of sales and expenditure for the period ahead and the resources to undertake this activity, a good deal of information about current performance and the reasons for this performance will have to be collected and analysed. Information about external influences in the marketplace as well as internal strengths and weaknesses will form the basis for the forecasts. Therefore a system is needed to capture this information and to enable the owner to extract and use it readily.

Question 3: What monitoring procedures and control systems will be needed to ensure that the business develops according to plan and that remedial action can be taken where it is needed?

Since it is difficult to predict exactly how the business will develop in the planning period (say up to three years), as many safeguards as possible should be installed so that management has full control over *cash* and *profit*. There are a number of procedures and systems that can relatively easily be implemented. Although they will not prevent poor decision-making, they should either act in a *preventative* way, so that the business does not get into trouble in the first place, or in a *curative* way, so that they provide information in time to take corrective action. We shall be discussing these two groups of measures in turn in chapter 5. Of course, everything costs money and proper financial management is no exception – the effort that goes into these procedures and systems is an investment in the long-term success of the business and, like any other kind of investment, the costs and benefits should be weighed up before taking action.

Objectives, scope and coverage

This book is written primarily for the owners of smaller businesses who are actively involved in the management of the business, either individually or in a management team, and who have some experience of financial management but little formal training. While the book is written from the point of view of the established small business, those who are in the process of setting up will also find it useful. This latter group will have to project themselves and their businesses to a point in the future where they might be able to relate the book's contents to their financial needs. This distinction is important because, when starting in business, it is impossible to imagine what kind of information might be required in the future. The owners of new businesses will not have much information to work with, but this should not stop them finding the book of practical use.

The book's general objective is to help people who run their own business to improve their understanding of financial management and accounting procedures. You will not be an expert already and will certainly not be a qualified financial manager, although you might unwittingly be performing this role amongst your many other roles.

There are several reasons for improving your understanding of financial management. First and foremost, you will want to improve the profitability of the business by introducing appropriate financial monitoring procedures and control systems. You might wish to present a plan to your bank manager, another financial institution or an individual investor, and the skills of putting together the figures and supporting detail will be an important determinant of whether you obtain the support you deserve. It is true that your accountant could do this for you, but where does this leave you when questions are asked about the contents of the plan? For those who wish to produce their own accounts or to be more confident in the presence of their accountant, this book should also be of help. In the final analysis, the production of the accounts should be left to the experts but, through an improvement in general knowledge of financial matters, you will be in a position to manage the business more effectively.

The remainder of this book is divided into five chapters.

Chapter 2 answers the question 'where is the business now?' and deals with profit and loss accounts, balance sheets and sources and applications of funds statements. We shall explain typical accounts for manufacturing and services/retail businesses and discuss the differences in the presentation of accounts between limited companies and unincorporated businesses.

Chapter 3 follows the discussion of financial accounts by applying them to an evaluation of financial and management performance over a given period of time. We shall discuss financial ratios and relationships that can easily be applied to any small business in order to work out how it has performed and where existing or potential problem areas are likely to emerge.

Chapter 4 answers the question 'where do you want the business to go to?' and deals with corporate planning, forecasting and budgeting methods and the information needed in order to produce realistic plans which can be monitored.

Chapter 5 answers the question 'what monitoring procedures and control systems will be needed to ensure that the plans are realized?' and deals with record-keeping, bookkeeping and management information and control systems. Accurate costing to ensure that each and every product or service that you sell makes its proper contribution to the overall profitability of the business is also covered. We shall attempt to take into account the needs of the more sophisticated growing business, but will cover procedures that even the smallest should be able to implement.

Chapter 6 recognizes that from time to time businesses need finance to survive and grow no matter how well they manage their existing resources and how expert they become at financial management. Indeed, it is knowing in good time that additional finance will be needed, and how much, that stamps the 'good financial management' seal of approval on the smaller business. This chapter deals with raising finance from the bank and other institutional and private sources.

In the field of education and self-improvement, the best way to learn is to do: the area of financial management is no exception. To test your understanding of the contents of each chapter, try to apply the knowledge gained to your own business and its financial accounting and management practices. Since we shall be using practical examples throughout, you should not find this difficult to do.

2

The financial statements

Outline

This chapter introduces you to your company's 'accounts'. At the end of it you will understand the key concepts and phrases that accountants use as well as the importance of:

- the profit and loss account
- the balance sheet
- the accounts of an unincorporated business
- the sources and application of funds statement

Financial statements of the affairs of the company (the 'accounts') must be prepared by every business (although there are differing legal requirements). It is our aim in this chapter to develop your understanding of the meaning of these financial accounts and their use as a tool in measuring the performance of your business. Accounts are prepared for a number of reasons:

(1) You will want to know how the business has *performed* over the year and what it is *worth* at the end of the year. Performance and worth are related: making more profit, which is then reinvested in the business (it either goes into the bank account as cash, or goes towards equipment or the running costs of the business), adds value and increases its net worth, which in turn increases the owner's worth. Even if profit is of little interest, you will want to measure how well the business has been managed. Of course, the accounts are already out of date when produced by the accountant, so you will ideally wish to construct regular monthly or quarterly accounts to guide the business through the year. Comparisons can be drawn against a number of yardsticks:

(a) the profit and loss accounts of previous years, which give a clear picture of how the business has changed over time in terms of sales and expenditure. For instance, you may wish to compare how expenditure on selling, promotional and distribution activities (the marketing costs) varies against sales income, since these form a large part of total expenditure and should show a more or less consistent pattern of change against sales over time.

(b) competitor performance or industry averages, since your competitors should have similar operating costs if their businesses are operated and managed like yours. If they make profits and you do not, you will be asking some serious questions about the way you run the business, which might be helpful in identifying problem areas and where improvements might be made.

(c) budgets and forecasts, which set out the financial picture based on your chosen strategy over the coming period. Actual profit and loss accounts can be compared with forecasts and differences (variances) identified, analysed and explained, allowing action to be taken to rectify unwanted deviations from the chosen path.

(2) Producing the accounts is important not only if you are thinking of selling the business, but also if you want to raise money: investors and lenders alike will be interested in the prospect of profits being distributed to shareholders and interest paid on loans. They will also be interested in business assets which are available as security for bank lending (these are to be found in the balance sheet).

(3) Legally, unincorporated businesses are obliged to produce annual accounts for the Inland Revenue, and limited companies for the Registrar of Companies, who will want to keep an eye on the affairs of the business (as prescribed by the Companies Act), and shareholders, who are entitled to know what has happened to their investment. The latter applies only to limited companies and not to sole traders and partnerships.

Companies are required to file a profit and loss account and balance sheet, an auditor's report and a director's report. Small companies can file modified accounts (abbreviated balance sheet and an auditor's report) if they satisfy two out of three of the following conditions:

not more than £2 million sales;
not more than £975000 total assets;
not more than 50 employees.

Medium-sized companies can also file modified accounts (abbreviated balance sheet and profit and loss account, auditor's report and director's report) if they satisfy two out of three of the following conditions:

not more than £8 million sales;

not more than £3.9 million total assets;

not more than 250 employees.

There are a number of concepts and conventions associated with the production of financial statements, which are universally agreed on by accountants as a way of maintaining consistency and comparability in accounting through the years. We shall meet the terms discussed below when we analyse the financial statements later:

1 *Realization*: sales income is taken into the business at the time of *invoicing* and not when the goods are ordered or paid for. Anything might go wrong in the interim and the income might never be received, but the remedy is to set off the bad debt as a deduction against income at a later stage. Thus invoiced sales are included when calculating profit, while payment received from your customers is a question of *cash flow*.
2 *Accrual*: costs accruing in a certain period must be matched to revenues in the same period. Thus when compiling the profit and loss account, costs associated with sales income must be included for that period (and not for any other period). An example would be the accountant's fees, which, although not billed to the business until some months after the end of the accounting period, are nevertheless included as an expenditure item in the annual accounts because they actually relate to that period.
3 *Money measurement*: only transactions which can be measured in monetary terms are included in the accounts. Where a monetary value cannot be assigned to something, such as people, it cannot appear in the accounts, since there is no way of assigning a value to it.
4 *Business entity*: the business is treated as an entity for the

purposes of drawing up accounts and is separate from its owners, employees or anyone else associated with it.

5 *Historical cost*: entries in the accounts are treated at their historic cost – what was actually paid for the item, rather than the current value if it were to be offered for sale. In certain cases, however, items may be revalued (such as buildings) but normally only for a specific purpose (such as when the business is being sold).

6 *Going concern*: the business is valued as a going concern, rather than on the basis of being broken up for sale.

7 *Dual aspect* of the balance sheet: entries show not only where money has come from but what it is being used for. Thus for every transaction, whether involving cash going out or cash coming in, there must be a balancing transaction.

8 *Conservatism*: profits are always understated rather than overstated. If there is any uncertainty about costs, they are always included at the higher level, while if sales are in doubt, they are always excluded.

9 *Materiality*: transactions are treated in a material way in the accounts. For instance, a pencil sharpener should be written off immediately as if it were revenue expenditure, rather than be treated as an item of capital expenditure (with its appropriate rate of depreciation).

10 *Consistency*: accounts are compiled on a consistent basis so that they can be compared through the course of time. If changes are to be introduced, for instance, in the way an asset is valued or depreciated, then the basis of the change should be noted explicitly.

We are now in a position to examine the accounts of two typical smaller companies in manufacturing and services and will observe the accounting conventions at work. Retail businesses will not differ much from these two types of businesses in the presentation of the accounts. There are some minor differences in the way that the profit and loss account and balance sheet are presented for limited companies and unincorporated businesses, because of their different tax treatments. They will be explained later.

The first company – Alcock's Joinery Limited – is a manufacturer of joinery products, selling direct to private households and, through architects and interior designers, to commercial customers. The second – SCS (Southern Computer Systems) Limited – is a supplier of computers, programs and accessories to larger engineering companies. Both companies are fictitious although we can easily imagine tens of thousands of companies exactly like them.

We have chosen two profitable companies which are not in any kind of trouble. They have both been making a profit over the past two years and both are growing, albeit at different rates: looking at the profit and loss accounts, the joinery company has grown very slowly, with sales up from £132898 to £154670, an increase of just 14 per cent and net profit before tax up by 78 per cent from £5087 to £9096; the computer company, in contrast has grown quite rapidly with sales up from £147158 to £225626, an increase of 53 per cent and net profit before tax up nearly seven times.

Turning to the balance sheets, the joinery company's net assets grew by 33 per cent over the year (from £14524 to £19375), whereas the computer company's grew by 62 per cent (from £26738 to £43281). We shall now discuss the two financial statements in detail, starting with the profit and loss accounts.

The profit and loss account

The profit and loss account is the 'history book' of the business – it tells us what has happened over the year to sales and expenditure and is therefore very revealing about how well the business has been managed. The profit and loss account shows how much net profit or loss the business has made during the year by recording, firstly, invoiced sales for the year and, secondly, invoiced expenditure associated with these sales. Businesses may offset against income all revenue expenditure incurred wholly and exclusively for business purposes plus capital allowances for expenditure on capital items (plant, equipment, machinery, motor vehicles). The period for which the profit and loss account is drawn up is normally 12 months, although at certain times (such as when a business starts) this period may be either longer or shorter. Certain types of business (such as retailers) may make up their profit and loss account on a 52 or 53 week basis. The period over which the accounts are drawn up is called the 'accounting period'.

Table 2.1 Alcock's Joinery Limited: profit and loss account for the year ending 31 March 1988

	1988 £	£	1987 £	£
Sales		154670		132898
Less: cost of sales				
Materials	35290		31045	
+ Opening stock and WIP	2130		1890	
	37420		32935	
− Closing stock and WIP	3790		2130	
	33630		30805	
Direct labour	46750		37400	
Subcontractors	9500		6350	
		89880		74555
		64790		58343
Selling/distribution expenses				
Travel and motor	6653		6579	
Advertising	4218		3709	
Administration expenses				
Rent and rates	10500		10500	
Light and heat	808		768	
Insurance	560		450	
Repairs and maintenance	962		1008	
Telephone	895		768	
Printing and stationery	1790		1670	
Postage	679		387	
General expenses	846		657	
Audit and accountancy	795		750	
Salaries and NIC	20560		19760	
Finance expenses				
Bank interest	1410		1424	
Bank charges	378		356	
Depreciation	4640	55694	4470	53256
Net profit		9096		5087
Taxation		2445		1831
Transferred to reserves		6651		3256

Table 2.2 Alcock's Joinery Limited: balance sheet at 31 March 1988

	1988 £	£	1987 £	£
FIXED ASSETS				
Equipment and machinery	39760		33685	
Motor vehicle	8900		8900	
	48660		42585	
Less: depreciation (1)	34091	14569	29451	13134
CURRENT ASSETS				
Stock and WIP	3790		2130	
Debtors	16863		13203	
Cash	3481		600	
	24134		15933	
Less: CURRENT LIABILITIES				
Trade creditors	6285		5188	
Sundry creditors	6295		4385	
Taxation	2445		1831	
Bank loan	1800		2563	
Overdraft	2503		576	
	19328		14543	
NET CURRENT ASSETS		4806		1390
NET ASSETS		19375		14524
Less: CREDITORS DUE AFTER MORE THAN ONE YEAR				
Bank loan		6114		7914
		13261		6610
FINANCED BY				
Share capital		2000		2000
Profit and loss account		11261		4610
		13261		6610

Note 1: Value of assets at cost	Equipment	Vehicle	Total
At 31 March 1987	33685	8900	42585
Acquired during year	6075	0	6075
At 31 March 1988	39760	8900	48660
Depreciation	@ 25%	@ 20%	
To 31 March 1987	23755	5696	29451
During year	4000	640	4640
To 31 March 1988	27755	6336	34091

Table 2.3 SCS (Southern Computer Systems) Limited: profit and loss account for the year ending 31 March 1988

	1988 £	£	1987 £	£
Sales		225626		147158
Less: cost of sales				
Purchases	82426		56905	
+ Opening stock and WIP	5130		9680	
	87556		66585	
− Closing stock and WIP	11275		5130	
		76281		61455
		149345		85713
Add: interest received		304		607
		149649		86320
Selling/distribution expenses				
Travel and subsistence	9103		6806	
Motor running costs	6181		3051	
Exhibitions	1834		1240	
Advertising	4365		2801	
Consultancy fees	2367		1456	
Administration expenses				
Rent and rates	8712		6307	
Light and heat	1628		891	
Insurance	927		821	
Repairs and maintenance	4016		1921	
Telephone	5876		4727	
Printing and stationery	1986		1670	
Postage	545		387	
General expenses	846		657	
Recruitment and training	456		234	
Audit and accountancy	975		456	
Salaries and NIC	57398		36910	
Directors' remuneration	4600		2350	
Finance expenses				
Leasing of cars	3690		2387	
Hire-purchase interest	735		599	
Bank interest	1720		438	
Bank charges	358		230	
Provision for bad debts	1345		0	
Depreciation	11975	131638	7132	83471
Net profit		18011		2849
Taxation		6757		1062
Transferred to reserves		11254		1787

Table 2.4 SCS (Southern Computer Systems) Limited: balance sheet at 31 March 1988

	1988 £	£	1987 £	£
FIXED ASSETS				
Equipment	23060		11270	
Motor vehicles	22580		12560	
Leasehold property	3560		3560	
Licences	15000		15000	
	64200		42390	
Less: depreciation (1)	31734	32466	19759	22631
CURRENT ASSETS				
Stock and WIP	11275		5130	
Debtors	46361		29028	
Cash	11415		82	
	69051		34240	
Less: **CURRENT LIABILITIES**				
Trade creditors	12420		9198	
Sundry creditors	10350		6025	
Hire purchase	2620		4892	
Taxation	6757		1062	
Overdraft	26089		8956	
	58236		30133	
NET CURRENT ASSETS		10815		4107
NET ASSETS		43281		26738
Less: **CREDITORS DUE AFTER MORE THAN ONE YEAR**				
Directors' loans	3025		3025	
Hire purchase	13345	16370	8056	11081
		26911		15657
FINANCED BY				
Share capital		10000		10000
Profit and loss account		16911		5657
		26911		15657

Note 1:	Equipment	Vehicles	Leases	Licences	Total
Value of assets at cost					
At 31 March 1987	11270	12560	3560	15000	42390
Acquired during year	11790	10020	0	0	21810
At 31 March 1988	23060	22580	3560	15000	64200
Depreciation	@ 25%	@ 20%	5 yrs	5 yrs	
To 31 March 1987	5850	2773	2136	9000	19759
During year	4302	3961	712	3000	11975
To 31 March 1988	10152	6734	2848	12000	31734

Sales income (or sales revenue, sales turnover)

Sales income, sales revenue and sales turnover are simply different words for the same transaction, namely invoiced sales in the period. In our examples, 1988 sales income for Alcock's Joinery was £154670 and for SCS, £225626. Note that sales are recorded when *invoiced*, regardless of whether customers have paid for them. This is the *realization concept* at work. The sales figure in the profit and loss account is taken from the sales day book (or if there is not one, from the analysed cash book, adjusted for sales receipts in other periods). Since VAT belongs to HM Government, the sales figure excludes output VAT.

Notice that the rate of sales growth differs between the two businesses: SCS has grown quite rapidly (53 per cent) whereas Alcock's has increased by only 17 per cent over the year. We shall observe the consequences of these differing growth rates in the next chapter.

Cost of sales (or cost of goods sold)

It is conventional to treat the *variable costs* of running the business before the *fixed costs*. In our examples, the term cost of sales is the variable cost – that is, it varies directly in proportion to changes in output or unit sales. This means that, if the business were to double its unit sales, it would expect to double (or more or less double) its cost of sales. The joinery company's cost of sales has grown by 20 per cent over the year (a little ahead of sales) and the computer company's by 25 per cent (considerably less than sales). Because of this, as a proportion of sales, the joinery company's cost of sales has risen from 56 per cent to 58 per cent over the year, whereas the computer company's cost of sales has fallen from 42 per cent to 34 per cent. Cost of sales includes the following:

(1) *Purchases* of raw materials, components, supplies or stock of any kind. Purchases must be adjusted for opening and closing stock and work in progress (WIP) before arriving at cost of sales. There is again no VAT in the figures. *Stock and work in progress* adjustments are required because, since the profit and loss account is produced on an accrued basis (see the *accrual concept* earlier), stock left over at

the end of the year does not match sales in that year. Because it must be matched, we adjust for stock by adding opening stock (stock brought forward from last year) and subtracting closing stock (stock carried forward to next year). This produces an adjusted purchases figure.

Stock is in the form of either raw materials or finished goods. Unfinished production yet to be invoiced is called work in progress. Stock is always valued at cost (or sometimes at net realizable value), after losses sustained through damage, theft or obsolescence have been deducted (in other words, what is really still useful to the business). Work in progress is valued at cost of materials and direct labour cost (production workers) plus a margin for overheads, and is often arrived at quite arbitrarily. Stock is normally physically *counted* to verify its existence and a comparison made against entries in the *stock control records*. In our examples, stock figures are quite low, although they are growing slowly.

(2) *Direct labour* associated with the production process, including subcontracted labour or production and freelance people brought in to design, make or provide goods or services. It is noticeable that the joinery company does have direct labour (skilled cabinet makers and joiners), whereas the computer company does not.

(3) Other variable costs or costs directly related to the production function, such as delivery costs and factory costs, including depreciation on factory machinery. These costs are normally included here if they can be separated from the remaining fixed costs of running the business. In practice, in the smaller business the two functions are essentially inseparable, and so we do not show them separately in our examples.

The purchases figure is taken from the purchases day book and represents the expenses invoiced to the business in the period and matched with the sales in that period, regardless of whether the bills have been paid (this is the *accrual concept* at work), or from the analysed cash book, with adjustments for payments in previous or future periods. Depreciation on production equipment and machinery will be calculated from entries in the fixed assets register or, if the business does not have one, will have to be calculated from equipment entries in the analysed cash book.

Gross profit

Gross profit is the profit remaining after deducting cost of sales from sales income. (The term *gross profit* is not actually used in the profit and loss account.) In the examples, gross profit as a percentage of sales (the *gross profit margin*) has risen from 58 per cent to 66 per cent in the case of the computer company (£85713 to £149345), but has fallen from 44 per cent to 42 per cent in the joinery company's accounts (£58343 to £64790). Notice that these percentages are the inverse of the cost of sales percentages we saw earlier.

Other income

Income from grants, interest or other sources is taken into the profit and loss account at this point. Since it does not relate to sales, it is not part of gross profit.

Overhead expenditure

It is conventional to treat the fixed costs (also called *overheads* or *operating costs*) of running the business in a logical order: first the sales and distribution expenses, followed by the administration expenses and finally the finance expenses.

Sales and distribution expenses

These are the costs of *marketing*: finding, getting and keeping customers, including the delivery of goods. Examples of sales and distribution expenses are media advertising, exhibitions, publicity, public relations, entertainment, printing of brochures and sales literature, postage and delivery of goods to customers, telephone calls, travel and subsistence related to sales, costs of employing sales and marketing staff including salaries and motor vehicles, commissions paid and any other costs directly associated with sales. In a small company it is difficult to differentiate most selling and general business expenses, such as travel (partly related to sales and partly to running the business), telephone and printing, and in these cases it is normal practice to combine them with general travel, telephone and printing expenses under administration expenses.

SCS appears to sell its computer systems mainly by travelling to see customers (it spent some £15000 on travel and motor expenses in 1988), and possibly as a result of leads generated from advertising and exhibitions (expenditure of about £6000). Marketing expenditure totalled £23850, equivalent to 10.6 per cent of sales, which was about equivalent to expenditure in 1987 (10.4 per cent).

Alcock's Joinery also appears to achieve its sales by visiting customers as a result of leads created by advertising. It probably has a more local marketplace than the computer company as marketing expenditure amounted to only 7 per cent of sales in 1988.

Sales and distribution expenditure is taken from the purchases day book (or from the adjusted analysed cash book).

Administration expenses

Administration expenses are the largest category of expenses in any business and are typically grouped into expenses associated with premises and other general running costs. The former include rent, rates, power, insurance, repairs and maintenance, and cleaning; general expenses include telephone, motoring, catering, printing and stationery, salaries, directors' remuneration, professional fees (including accountancy and audit), recruitment and training, etc. Salaries and remuneration include employer's National Insurance contributions (NIC). Note that business entertainment expenses (as well as any other expenses not necessary for the business) are not an allowable expense for tax purposes and will be added back before arriving at taxable income.

In our examples, administration expenses were a typically high proportion of sales: £87965 (39 per cent) in the case of SCS and £38395 (25 per cent) for Alcock's Joinery. The largest contributors to administration expenses are rent and salaries. In the rapidly growing computer business, salaries and directors' remuneration (£61998) accounted for 27 per cent of sales in 1988 and grew by 58 per cent over the year (up from £39260).

Like all the other expenses, administration is taken from the purchases day book (or from the adjusted analysed cash book) and excludes VAT.

Finance expenses

The costs of financing the business are covered under this heading and include interest paid on bank loans, overdrafts and hire-purchase agreements, leasing and hire charges, and bank charges. In some businesses depreciation is grouped under finance expenses. It is conventional to list finance expenses separately because the business can be financed in different ways at different points in time (combinations of equity, loans and off-balance-sheet finance). Performance should be analysed independently of the financing of the business in order to compare more accurately performance in previous years or against competitors.

Note that repayments of borrowings to the bank or to hire-purchase companies are not an expense item and are therefore not included in the profit and loss account (although they are included in cash flow and the balance sheet). Like the other expenses above, finance expenses are taken from the purchases day book (or the analysed cash book).

Finance expenses can be an enormous drain on the profits of a business. In our examples, however, they seem quite modest. Alcock's Joinery paid a small amount of interest and bank charges (£1788) amounting to 1 per cent of sales; SCS paid relatively more at 3 per cent of sales (£6503) and appears to have used several methods of financing the business, namely leasing, hire purchase and bank loans. We shall observe how these financing methods contribute to the stability of the business when we discuss the balance sheet below.

Provision for bad debts

The computer business has a debt from a customer (£1345) which could be irrecoverable. By providing for the likelihood that the customer will not settle the outstanding debt (the reasons are numerous, although typically there is a dispute about the amount or the customer is in financial difficulties), the net profit reflects reality more accurately. Note that for *tax purposes*, however, this provision will not count as an allowable expense and will be added back before arriving at taxable income. Only bad debts proved to be irrecoverable (such as when the customer has been officially wound up) are allowable.

Depreciation

There is only one remaining expense item that has not been recovered from sales. It is the cost of purchasing capital assets, such as equipment and machinery. We need a way of treating the purchase of these assets because, unlike all the other expenses discussed so far, which are of a recurrent nature, capital assets typically have a life of more than one year. The accounting concept that spreads the cost of plant, equipment, machinery, motor vehicles, buildings and other assets over their useful lives is called *depreciation*. The confusing thing about depreciation is that it does not involve a movement of cash (that is, setting aside money).

A simple example will demonstrate how depreciation is calculated, using the 'straight-line' method. A machine costing £5000 has a useful life of five years (in other words, at the end of the fifth year it will be worth nothing and will have to be replaced). Assuming that the asset is 'used up' in equal amounts each year, depreciation is calculated by dividing the cost of the asset (£5000) by its useful life (five years), which gives an annual depreciation of £1000. Thus at the end of the fifth year, the *book value* of the asset will be zero. This does not necessarily mean that the machine has no residual value, but rather that it has been 'written off' completely in the books.

Alternatively, depreciation can be calculated by using the 'reducing-balance' method, whereby a fixed percentage is applied to the balance at the end of each year. The percentage is related to the 'useful life' concept and is meant to be more realistic in that it recognizes that new assets decline in value more rapidly in the early years and seldom reach zero value in the books of account. For example, depreciation of the same machine at a rate of 20 per cent over five years would result in a residual book value, as follows:

Cost of machine	£5000
Depreciation year 1 (20%)	£1000
Book value beginning year 2	£4000
Depreciation year 2 (20%)	£800

Book value beginning year 3	£3200
Depreciation year 3 (20%)	£640
Book value beginning year 4	£2560
Depreciation year 4 (20%)	£512
Book value beginning year 5	£2048
Depreciation year 5 (20)%	£410
Book value beginning year 6	£1638

According to the *straight-line method* of depreciation, the machine would have zero value in the books, with total depreciation over the period (£5000) exactly equalling the original cost. According to the *reducing-balance method*, the machine stands in the books at a value of £1638 at the end of five years, after a cumulative depreciation of £3362. The chosen method will depend on the likelihood of there being a residual value or not at the end of the useful life of the machine.

In our examples, depreciation amounted to £4640 for Alcock's Joinery and to £11975 for SCS. Exactly how these amounts are calculated will depend on the nature of capital assets acquired over the period and the rate of depreciation used in each case. Different assets will attract different rates of depreciation because in real life they will, in fact, suffer different rates of wear and tear. In order to calculate depreciation, we need to know what has been purchased over the period. This is revealed, in practice, in notes to the accounts following the balance sheet, so we shall return to the calculation of depreciation once we have introduced the balance sheet. The rate of depreciation is a decision for the business owner and is normally taken in consultation with the firm's accountant, but it should reflect what happens in real life.

The amount of depreciation taken into the profit and loss account in a year, being an arbitrary decision, is not an allowable expense for tax purposes and will be added back before arriving at taxable income. It should not be confused with *capital allowances*, which are what the government is prepared to allow the business to write down against its taxable income in lieu of the purchase of items of plant, equipment, machinery and motor vehicles. While depreciation rates might differ according to the asset in question, capital allowances are fixed at 25 per cent on most items of plant, equipment and machinery (although in certain parts of the United Kingdom, such as Enterprise Zones, the rate is 100 per cent).

Depreciation is an expense item in the accounts even when the asset in question is *appreciating* in value. The concepts of conservatism and consistency are demonstrated here: it is normally very difficult to forecast how the value of business assets (such as land and buildings) might change over time, and so it is prudent to assume that they will have to be replaced at some stage out of profits.

Depreciation does not normally compensate completely for the *replacement cost* of an asset, since amounts are stated in the accounts at historical cost (what was paid for the asset in question) and not at current prices (which are bound to be considerably above historical cost). This will almost certainly require the business to finance the renewal of the asset partly out of additional profits made over the period.

Net profit

Net profit is an important measure of performance and is what remains after deducting overheads from gross profit. Alcock's Joinery experienced a marked improvement in profit over the year (from £5087 to £9096) to a net profit on sales of 5.8 per cent. SCS showed a large gain in profitability over the period, up from £2849 to £18011 (8 per cent of sales).

Taxation

Corporation tax at 25 per cent on the ordinary activities of the business is normally shown at this point in the profit and loss account, although the calculation, based on adjusted net profit after adding back disallowable expenses (such as entertainment and depreciation) and deducting capital allowances, is a matter of confidence between the business and its advisors. Both our companies were liable for corporation tax: Alcock's Joinery for £2445 and SCS for £6757.

Extraordinary items

Extraordinary items of expenditure are taken into account at this point. Because they are normally exceptional items (they are unlikely to occur again), they are not regarded as part of ordinary trading. They are then taxed in the normal way. Neither of the businesses showed extraordinary items of expenditure. An example would be legal charges associated with a particular activity (such as a court action) which is unlikely to be repeated.

Dividends

Dividends are a distribution of profit to shareholders and are included at this point. Neither business declared a dividend. The decision to do so is dependent on profit and is at the discretion of the directors. The advantage of declaring a dividend in a private company is that the distribution does not attract employer's National Insurance contributions; the disadvantage is that advance corporation tax (ACT) is payable.

Retained profit

At last, the final line in the profit and loss account! The amount left over after post-tax distributions is called *retained profit* (known as 'the bottom line') and is transferred to reserves in the balance sheet. In this way, the profit and loss account and the balance sheet are linked. In 1988 Alcock's Joinery had a retained profit of £6651 and that of SCS was £11254.

The balance sheet

Unlike the profit and loss account (the 'history book'), the balance sheet is made up at a point in time and is therefore rather like a 'photograph', showing what the business owes to others (liabilities) and what it owns or is owed (assets). The excess of what the business owns over what it owes to others is called *net worth* and the balance sheet's importance lies in being able to define this amount. Net worth is important because it represents the (book) value to the shareholders of their interest in the business. If you are the owner or major shareholder in the business, then clearly you should be interested in its net worth. The balance sheet also contains a number of other features, such as how the resources have been utilized and, in combination with the profit and loss account, how well managed and stable the business is.

The balance sheet represents only items to which monetary values can be assigned (the *money measurement* concept), which in practice limits its relevance, since the worth to the business of the directors, managers and employees cannot be represented. A further limitation lies in the fact that the book value of the assets (what they are worth in the books of account after deducting depreciation from the original cost) does not properly reflect what the business is really worth on the open market. The assets themselves may be worth considerably less than their stated value, particularly in the event of a forced sale (such as when the business is wound up). Thus the notion of 'net worth' has limited practical meaning.

Balance sheets are conventionally laid out to show the net worth of the business and the financing of this worth. By definition, balance sheets must balance, so that what the business owns is balanced by what it owes. We start by looking at what the business owns (the assets) and move on to what it owes (the liabilities). As with the profit and loss account, the balance sheet shows the current year (1988) on the left-hand side with the previous year (1987) on the right.

Fixed assets

The first items are the most enduring assets owned by the business. They are called *fixed assets*, the capital items with a life of more than 12 months that help to generate income and profit. They are normally divided into *tangible assets*, such as land, buildings, plant, equipment and machinery, motor vehicles and fixtures and fittings, *intangible assets*, such as licences, patents, goodwill, leases and major development costs, and *investments* in other companies.

Fixed assets are stated in the balance sheet at cost (the *cost concept*) and depreciated cumulatively over their useful life to show their net book value. Fixed assets are itemized in a *fixed assets register* where depreciation is recorded against each asset over its life. (Very few small businesses keep a detailed register of fixed assets and as a result there is usually no exact record of the equipment, machinery, tools and vehicles owned by the business.) Alcock's Joinery had fixed assets worth £48660 at cost, which included equipment and machinery worth £39760 and a vehicle worth £8900. The difference of £6075 between 1987 and 1988 is represented by the purchase of additional equipment. SCS not only had equipment (£23060) and vehicles (£22580) in its balance sheet, but also a leasehold property (they probably paid £3560 as a premium for the lease) and licences which cost them £15000 (the licences probably represent the amount paid to other software companies for the use of their proprietary software). The differences between 1987 and 1988 (equipment worth £11790 and motor vehicles worth £10020) represent the company's investment in additional productive capacity. No new leasehold property or licences were taken on during the year.

Depreciation

Depreciation appears again in the balance sheet, but in a slightly different guise. Different rates of depreciation are applied to different assets, depending on their useful life, and a full explanation of depreciation charges must be given in the accounts. In our examples, aggregate cumulative depreciation is set against total fixed assets (in 1988 cumulative depreciation was £31734 for SCS and £34091 for Alcock's Joinery) leaving a net book value of £32466 and £14569 respectively. 'Cumulative' depreciation means that the depreciation of successive years is added together to give a running total in the balance sheet. This is illustrated below.

Note 1 in the balance sheet refers us to the detail at the end of the page, where the aggregate value of the assets at cost and the associated depreciation are shown. We are shown exactly how much cumulative depreciation was set against each type of asset up to the end of the previous year (1987) and during the 1988 financial year at the relevant rate of depreciation according to the type of asset. This should reflect the lives of the assets in question: both equipment (25 per cent per annum) and vehicles (20 per cent per annum) are depreciated on a *reducing-balance basis*, whereas leases and licences are depreciated on a *straight-line basis* over their life. (From this we can deduce that the lease has five years to run to the next rent review and the licence is valid for a period of five years.)

Depreciation shown in the profit and loss account is for the current year only, whereas in the balance sheet it is shown cumulatively (from the moment the asset was purchased, no matter how long ago, up to the current balance sheet year end). To demonstrate how annual depreciation is calculated, equipment in SCS's balance sheet is used as an example:

Value of equipment at cost to 31/3/87	£11270
Cumulative depreciation to 31/3/87	£5850
Net book value of equipment at 31/3/87	£5420
Equipment acquired during year to 31/3/88	£11790
Value of equipment used during year	£17210
Depreciation at 25% (reducing balance)	£4302

The same calculation (at 20 per cent) produces depreciation for vehicles (£3961), while the leases and licences are depreciated by equal amounts over their remaining lives (£712 and £3000 respectively). The sum of these four amounts appears in the profit and loss account as depreciation for the year; table 2.4 shows how cumulative depreciation (£31734) is calculated, by adding the amount for the year (£11975) to the accumulated amount up to the 31 March of the previous year (£19759).

Current assets

Current assets have a life of less than 12 months and include, in ascending order of liquidity, stock and work in progress, debtors, deposits and prepayments (to other people), and cash. Cash is the most liquid current asset, whereas stock is the least liquid (it still has to be sold). Debtors falls in the middle, having been sold but not yet turned into cash. Alcock's Joinery had current assets of £24134 in 1988 (up by 51 per cent from £15933) and SCS had current assets of £69051 (up by 102 per cent from £34240).

Stock and work in progress is the closing amount that appeared in the profit and loss account and is a current asset because it is owned by the business and will shortly (within the next few months) be sold to produce cash. Alcock's Joinery had a very low level of stock and work in progress in 1988 (£3790), probably comprising mostly timber and other consumable goods; SCS had a higher level (£11275), probably development work on computer software systems.

Debtors (money owed by customers) includes VAT and is taken from the nominal ledger (which summarizes the sales ledger) or from the 'unpaid invoices' file. Debtors are current assets because they are owed to the business and will be paid within the next few months. Alcock's Joinery had debtors of £16863 in 1988; SCS had debtors of £46361.

Prepayments or deposits include rent deposits and prepayments on orders. Technically they are current assets because the business still owns the payments and will have them repaid at an agreed future time, or goods and services will be received for them at some point. Neither of our examples had prepayments or deposits.

Cash includes petty cash and cash on all current and short-term deposit accounts, and is recorded in the petty cash book, cash book and other records of monies on deposit. Alcock's Joinery had cash resources of £3481 and SCS had £11415. Note that cash at the bank is *not* the same as net profit after taxation: the profit and loss accounts of the two companies demonstrate this clearly. Although it is true to say that the increase in profits in both examples could have resulted in an increase in cash on deposit, the financial statements need further analysis before we can be conclusive about the source of the additional cash.

Current liabilities

Current liabilities are amounts due by the business to its creditors within the following 12 months. They include trade creditors, sundry creditors (amounts owed to the Inland Revenue and VAT), income and corporation taxes owed, prepayments and deposits (by customers), hire purchase and bank loans repayable within the next 12 months and the overdraft. In 1988 Alcock's current liabilities grew from £14543 to £19328 (an increase of 33 per cent) and SCS's grew very rapidly from £30133 to £58236 (an increase of 93 per cent).

Trade creditors records the as yet unpaid amounts supplied on credit to the business by the trade. The business will have taken delivery but will have been given a certain period of credit by the supplier: in effect, the business is using its trade suppliers as a short-term source of finance. Creditors are clearly a liability since they are amounts owed by the business. They are normally recorded in the nominal ledger or in the 'awaiting payment' file. Alcock's Joinery had trade creditors of £6285 in 1988 and SCS had £12420.

Sundry creditors includes PAYE owed to the Inland Revenue (currently PAYE amounts outstanding at the end of the month must be paid by the nineteenth of the following month) and VAT to Customs and Excise (which must be paid within one month of the end of the VAT period). PAYE owed is recorded in the salaries and wages book or in the deductions working sheets, and VAT is recorded in a separate VAT account which all businesses are required to keep. In our examples, Alcock's had sundry creditors of £6295 in 1988, and SCS had £10350.

Taxation includes tax assessed and payable within the next 12 months either for Schedule D income (unincorporated businesses only) or for companies paying corporation tax under the Income and Corporation Taxes Act. Tax payable is based on adjusted net profit (see the profit and loss account earlier), and in the examples Alcock's is due to pay £2445 and SCS, £6757.

Hire purchase and bank loans due for repayment within the next 12 months are recorded as current liabilities. Since hire-purchase facilities and bank loans are normally made available over a period of several years, only the amounts due within the next 12 months are recorded here, and the balances due for repayment later are recorded as long-term liabilities (creditors due after more than one year) in the balance sheet. Outstanding hire-purchase amounts and bank loans are recorded separately in a loans register. Alcock's Joinery had a bank loan of which £1800 was due to be repaid in the year to March 1989; SCS had hire-purchase facilities of which £2620 was due for repayment in the coming year.

The *overdraft* is the amount overdrawn at the bank at the close of the financial year and is recorded in the cash book (reconciled with the bank statement). The overdraft is a current liability since it is short-term borrowing agreed for a period of up to 12 months and is normally renegotiated for the next year, in line with cash flow requirements. In the examples, both companies increased their overdrafts: Alcock's increased only marginally to £2503, but SCS jumped from £8956 to £26089. There is no contradiction in there being *cash* in the balance sheet as well as an *overdraft* (both our examples show this phenomenon) since one or both amounts could be temporary situations only, reflecting a sudden change in the movement of cash into or out of the business.

Net current assets (or liabilities)

Current liabilities are subtracted from current assets to give net current assets. (If current liabilities were larger than current assets, the result would be net current liabilities.) This excess – the short-term amount owing to the business after short-term debts are repaid – is also called *working capital*, and has to be financed from appropriate sources, typically from the overdraft or other short-term instruments. Alcock's Joinery had net current assets of £4806 and SCS had £10815. Both companies thus increased their working capital requirements over the period.

Net assets

Net assets is the sum of fixed assets and net current assets. From the point of view of how financial resources are used in the business, we can restate the net assets position as follows: by adding fixed capital (which we called fixed assets earlier) to working capital (which we called net current assets earlier), we arrive at total capital employed (or net assets). In our examples, Alcock's had total capital (net assets) of £19328 and SCS had capital of £43281.

These alternative names for the same amounts (fixed assets or fixed capital, net current assets or working capital and net assets or total capital invested) are a reflection of the different uses and meanings of the balance sheet. In this case, we can either think in terms of what the business owns (assets) and owes to others (liabilities), or in terms of where the finance is invested (fixed and working capital) and whence it comes (capital employed).

Creditors due after more than one year

We turn now to the long-term liabilities of the business, also known as capital employed. The rest of the balance sheet comprises the sources of long-term capital which are customarily separated into long-term loans of various kinds (treated first) and the amounts belonging to the shareholders (treated second).

Long-term creditors include bank loans, commercial mortgages, hire-purchase facilities, directors' loans and deferred income or corporation tax. Loans outstanding and hire-purchase agreements should be recorded in a separate loans register.

Bank loans include term loans of two years or more and commercial mortgages. The amounts repayable within the next 12 months are recorded under current liabilities in the balance sheet (see above), and so only the amounts owing over the longer period are recorded here. In our examples, Alcock's had a bank loan of £6114 outstanding at the end of 1988 after repaying £1800 of the principal sum over the year (in 1987 the amount outstanding was £7914).

Directors' loans are loans from directors to the business and are normally made available for more than 12 months. The reason that directors lend money to the business (rather than invest in the share capital) is that there are no tax penalties in withdrawing it at a later stage. Only SCS had directors' loans (£3025). Directors' loans are recorded in a loans register.

Hire-purchase is the amount owing to hire-purchase companies after the next 12 months (amounts repayable within the next 12 months are recorded under current liabilities) and includes capital and interest repayments. SCS had hire-purchase facilities of £13345 outstanding in 1988, up from £8056 in 1987, which reflects the increased use of this method of financing the company's growth. Like the company's other borrowings, hire purchase is recorded in a loans register.

Deferred taxation is included as a long-term creditor if it is payable after a 12 month period (neither of our examples has deferred tax). Unincorporated businesses paying income tax under Schedule D would normally have deferred taxation, since unincorporated businesses are taxed on a preceding year basis (and so tax is paid a year later).

Net worth

Net worth is a term not explicitly used in the balance sheet. It represents what the business is worth *after all creditors* have been repaid (with the exception of shareholders); thus what remains belongs exclusively to the shareholders or, in other words, the proprietors of the business. This is why it is so important. It is calculated by subtracting long-term creditors from net assets. In our examples, Alcock's had a net worth of £13261 in 1988:

net assets	£19375
– bank loan	£6114
net worth	£13261

SCS had a net worth of £26911:

net assets	£43281
– directors' loans	£3025
– hire purchase	£13345
net worth	£26911

Capital and reserves (financed by)

The most permanent capital in the business is supplied by the shareholders and it is solely for the shareholders that profit is made. Included under this heading are long-term sources of finance: paid-up share capital, share premium, revaluation reserve and accumulated profit or loss.

Share capital (or owner's funds in an unincorporated business) is the owner's investment. A distinction must be made between *paid-up* share capital and issued but not yet paid-up capital. Only the former is normally shown in the balance sheet of a small company, since this represents the amount actually paid by the shareholders into the bank account. In return, they will be issued share certificates as evidence of their shareholdings. Alcock's has paid-up share capital of £2000 and SCS has £10000. (It is quite common for small companies to have the minimum possible paid-up share capital of £2.)

Share premium arises where the shares are sold to shareholders above their par value (at a premium). For instance, if 100 £1 shares in a company were sold for £1.50 each, the share premium would be £0.50 per share, or a total of £50. This premium would be shown in the balance sheet. There are no share premiums in either of our examples.

Revaluation reserve arises where fixed assets are revalued at current market prices (or any amount above their historical cost). A typical case would be the revaluation of a freehold building: normally the building would be stated in the balance sheet at cost (the purchase price), but at some point in time it could be deemed appropriate to revalue the asset at current market price. Since a balance sheet has to balance, any change in the value of the building at one end of the balance sheet must require a balancing entry at another point. In this case, the entry is shown at this point. For example, if one of our companies owned its building outright (say it purchased the building for £100000), this would be shown in the balance sheet as a fixed asset. Now if the owners decided to revalue the building at its true market price (say £200000), because they wished to sell the company, fixed assets would rise to £200000 and a revaluation reserve of £100000 would be shown in the balance sheet. In the event, neither of our examples has revalued any of its assets.

Profit and loss account is the amount accumulated from successive profit and loss accounts since the company started. In this way, profit builds up capital in the business while loss reduces capital. Alcock's showed accumulated profit of £11261 (up from £4610), which is calculated in the following way:

accumulated profit 1987	£4610
transferred to reserves 1988	£6651
accumulated profit 1988	£11261

SCS had accumulated profit in 1988 of £16911 (up from £5657).

The balance

Finally, since a balance sheet must balance, share capital and profit must equal net worth. In Alcock's case:

share capital	£2000
profit	£11261
total shareholders' interest	£13261

This is the same as net worth: net assets (£19375) minus bank loan (£6114).

In SCS's case:

share capital	£10000
profit	£16911
total shareholders' interest	£26911

This is the same as net worth: net assets (£43281) minus directors' loans and hire purchase (£16370).

Presentation of accounts for sole traders and partnerships

For tax purposes, the accounts of unincorporated businesses are presented somewhat differently. The difference arises because a limited company is a separate person in law and it employs the owners (shareholders), who, being employees, have to pay tax under Schedule E of the Income and Corporation Taxes Act (they are liable to deductions under PAYE). However, in an unincorporated business, the owners are not separate from the business and their remuneration is therefore treated as part of profit.

In the profit and loss account, the proprietors' remuneration is called *drawings* (not salaries). Drawings are not included as an item of expenditure (as salaries are), but are treated as part of profit. Using Alcock's as an example, assume that the business is not a limited company and that there is one owner. The profit and loss account would differ from the earlier version in the following ways:

1 Under *administration expenses*, the amount for *salaries and NIC* would change. Salaries for employed staff would be entered at this point in the normal way, but the owner's remuneration (drawings) would be excluded.

2 *Net profit* would therefore be greater as the owner's drawings have not yet been deducted. This is the last line in the profit and loss account.

3 *Taxation* and *reserves* would not appear at all at this point in an unincorporated business.

If Alcock's were a partnership (not a sole trader), net profit would be apportioned between the partners in proportion to their agreed shares of the profit.

In the case of the balance sheet shown in table 2.5, there are further changes from the layout presented earlier (the following changes are annotated on the balance sheet):

1 *Cash* tends to be larger in the unincorporated business (for identical situations) because of unpaid tax.

Table 2.5 Alcock's Joinery: balance sheet at 30 April 1988

	£	£
FIXED ASSETS		
Equipment and machinery	39760	
Motor vehicle	8900	
	48660	
Less: depreciation	34091	14569
CURRENT ASSETS		
Stock and WIP	3790	
Debtors	16863	
Cash (1)	9481	
	30134	
Less: CURRENT LIABILITIES		
Trade creditors	6285	
Sundry creditors	6295	
Taxation (2)	3560	
Bank loan	1800	
Overdraft	2503	
	20443	
NET CURRENT ASSETS		9691
NET ASSETS		24260
Less: CREDITORS DUE AFTER MORE THAN ONE YEAR		
Bank loan	6114	
Taxation (3)	4670	10784
		13476
FINANCED BY (4)		
Capital account brought forward		12598
Profit and loss account		21108
		33706
Drawings		12000
		21706
Taxation		8230
		134760

2 *Taxation* would not represent unpaid corporation tax, as an unincorporated business pays income tax on a preceding year basis. Thus the tax shown here, payable on 1 January and 1 July each year, would be the assessed tax for the previous accounting period.

3 Additional *taxation* would be shown under *creditors due after more than one year*, representing the amount of tax payable next year (on the profits made this year).

4 *Financed by* would include *owner's capital account* (like share capital) brought forward from the previous balance sheet, as well as any amounts introduced during the year, *profit* for the year from the profit and loss account, *drawings* in the period and *taxation* owed, both in the current year and for the following year (the total of 2 and 3 above).

This is an example of Alcock's balance sheet presented as if it were a sole trader (1988 only shown here). If Alcock's were a partnership, each partner's capital account would be shown separately in the same way as the single proprietor's is shown in table 2.5, with each partner's share of the profit, drawings and taxation treated in the same way.

Sources and applications of funds statement

Our final financial statement looks very carefully at the way that finance has been used by the business over the past year. The sources and applications of funds statement reveals from which sources the business has drawn its funding over the year (sources) and to what purpose these funds have been applied (applications). The principal reason for wishing to analyse sources and applications is to discover whether the business has used its available finance efficiently and whether the fundamental canons of finance have been observed, namely that long-term capital matches assets with a long-term life, and that short-term capital matches short-term needs.

The reason for this principle is that long-term finance (share capital, profits, term loans, hire purchase, mortgages) is available over a number of years and therefore should be used to invest in assets (plant, equipment, vehicles, buildings) which will earn profits over a number of years; short-term finance (trade credit, overdraft) is only available for a short period (typically a few months in the case of trade credit and up to a year in the case of the overdraft) and therefore should only cover short-term needs (debtors, stock). If short-term finance were to be withdrawn at short notice (suppliers not allowing credit or the bank calling in the overdraft), at least only short-term needs would be in jeopardy and possibly alternative sources could be found. But if short-term finance (overdraft) were being applied to long-term needs (machinery), calling in the overdraft would affect the business in two ways: firstly, by requiring it to sell assets to raise cash and, secondly, by removing support for working capital and running costs, thus forcing the business into a position where it could not meet its daily outgoings.

The sources and applications of funds statement uses existing figures from the profit and loss account (1988) and balance sheets (1987 and 1988): no new work is required. Most of the figures entered in the sources and applications of funds statement represent the differences between the balance sheets at two different points in time: in this case, the balance sheets at 31 March 1987 and 31 March 1988. The statement (table 2.6), using SCS as an example, sets out the long-term sources of funds first, then goes on to list the long-term applications, and finally reviews short-term applications and sources simultaneously.

Internal sources are treated first. *Profit before tax* (£18011) was taken from the profit and loss account for 1988, since profit is a long-term source of finance. There was an adjustment for *depreciation* (£11975), which does not involve any physical movement of funds (it is a notional concept only), by adding back the amount for the year. Depreciation, like profit, is regarded as a source of funds.

External sources included *sale of fixed assets*, additional *shares* and *loans* in the year (of which there were none), additional *hire purchase* (up from £8056 to £13345, an increase of £5289), additional *directors' loans* (they remained unchanged) and *taxation* (up from £1062 to £6757, an increase of £5695). Unpaid taxation is a source of funds until such time as it is paid to the Inland Revenue. Internal and external sources amounted to £40970.

Turning to long-term applications, most of the funds went into *purchases of fixed assets* (up from £42390 to £64200, an increase of

Table 2.6 SCS Limited: sources and applications of funds for the year ending 31 March 1988

	£
SOURCES	
Internal	
Profit before tax	18011
Adjustment: depreciation	11975
Total internal	29986
External	
Sale of fixed assets	–
Share issue	–
Long-term loans	–
Hire purchase	5289
Directors' loans	0
Taxation	5695
Total external	10984
Internal and external (a)	40970
APPLICATIONS	
Purchase of fixed assets	21810
Long-term loans repaid	–
Hire purchase repaid	2272
Directors' loans repaid	0
Tax paid	6757
Dividends paid	–
Total applications (b)	30839
EXCESS OF LONG-TERM FUNDS (a)–(b)	10131
NET MOVEMENT IN WORKING CAPITAL	
Stock and work in progress	6145
Debtors	17333
(Creditors)	(7547)
Total (c)	15931
NET MOVEMENT IN LIQUID FUNDS	
Cash	11333
Overdraft	(17133)
Total (d)	(5800)
NET DEFICIT IN WORKING CAPITAL (c)–(d)	10131

£21810). There were no *long-term loans repaid*, *hire purchase repaid* amounted to £2272 (£4892 to £2620), there were no *directors' loans repaid*, *tax paid* amounted to £6757 (from the profit and loss account) and there were no *dividends*. Applications of funds amounted to £30839, leaving an excess of sources over applications of £10131. What has happened to this excess?

Movements in short-term funds are examined next. *Working capital* increased by £15931, made up of increases of £6145 in *stock and work in progress* (up from £5130 to £11275), £17333 in *debtors* (up from £29028 to £46361) and (as a short-term source of funds) £7547 in total creditors (up from £15223 to £22770). The increase in working capital was partly funded by an increase in liquid funds of £5800 (cash balances rose by £11333 but were balanced by an increase in the overdraft from £8956 to £26089). Thus the deficit in working capital funding was £10131, which was met by the excess of long-term sources. The amounts must balance exactly, since they originate in the profit and loss account and balance sheet, which, by definition, must balance.

Financial accounting is a technical subject but its understanding is critical to an examination of business performance. We have seen how profit contributes to the overall financing of the business and how cash is generated as a result of the accumulation of profit. The financial accounts presented in this chapter provide a clear picture of how the two businesses have performed over the year and we can now go on to examine and analyse this performance, in order to identify where profits have come from and what improvements might be made.

Key points

- The Profit and Loss Account is a 'history book' revealing how the business has performed over the year.
- The Balance Sheet is a 'photograph' detailing what the business owes and owns, and therefore what it is worth, and the way it is financed.
- The importance of the sources and applications of funds statement lies in the way it identifies how the business has utilized available funds in the year.
- The accounts are drawn up conservatively: sales should not be overstated and costs should not be understated.

3

Measuring financial performance

Outline

This chapter shows you how to apply financial ratios to the various accounts you have encountered in chapter 2 to evaluate the performance of your business. The four key ratios are:

- profitability ratios
- financial status ratios
- financial management ratios
- resource management ratios

We are now in a position to use the financial accounts to evaluate performance. The appropriate question to ask is: 'How well have the two companies performed over the period under review?' Our aim in this chapter is to review all the relevant financial ratios that will allow you to analyse your own performance and ultimately to use as an aid in forecasting your accounts.

Before proceeding to an answer, there are a number of issues relevant to company performance for discussion: the 'caveats', so to speak. In the world of small business, there is no need to go to extreme lengths to analyse the performance of a company when the shareholders are the people who own and manage the business. Sophisticated methods of analysis are the preserve of the much larger, usually publicly quoted, company, where there is sufficient information available to produce meaningful analyses. The smaller company does not generally provide detailed financial information about its performance to the interested outsider and the information required internally to make the right business decisions is all that really matters.

Notwithstanding this limitation, there is good reason for the smaller company to take heed of the elements of financial performance analysis. Not only would they be useful in comparing performance against some agreed yardstick (such as a budget), but, certain outsiders, such as bankers, suppliers and landlords, would be using performance indicators to help with lending, supply and renting decisions respectively.

Current performance is normally measured against that of previous years as well as that of competitors (or industry averages). In the case of smaller companies, there is little relevant information publicly available about the performance of competitors, and even those few figures that are published are either out of date or not of similar types of companies. So whereas a whole information industry has been built on the publication of inter-company comparisons, it is mainly representative of and relevant to larger established companies.

This leaves previous years' figures as the most salient yardstick against which to measure current performance, although trends in the industry in general terms should always be borne in mind before arriving at conclusions. Thus if your business has performed particularly badly, while the industry in general has gone from strength to strength, you would be hard-pressed to convince an observer that your performance was due to factors beyond your control (although this might be the case). Some knowledge of industry performance is a necessary requirement for evaluating the performance of individual businesses, for there must be a general yardstick against which to assess progress. Industry performance standards are generally available through membership of industry organizations or from published government statistics, such as the Business Monitor series (HMSO).

Using financial ratios to measure performance

There are a number of measures of performance in four key areas of the business, i.e. *overall profitability, financial status, management of finance* and *management of resources*. We shall use our earlier examples to illustrate the use of key ratios in analysing performance but we shall have to qualify our conclusions, as with only two years' accounts available, we shall not always be in a position to form an unequivocal view. When evaluating company performance, there should be at least five years' history available in order to ensure that atypical years do not form the basis of assessment and that trends can be established over a sufficient period of time. As a preliminary step, therefore, it would be wise to have available five years' profit and loss accounts and five years' balance sheets. Some preparation will almost certainly be involved here, unless your accounts have been prepared with a view to the analysis of comparative performance. We return to the question of preparation in chapter 4.

Profitability ratios

Profitability ratios are arguably the most important ratios since they reveal much about return to the risk takers (the shareholders) and the possible reasons for variations in these returns. Profitability ratios are normally compared with previous years' figures, industry averages, alternative forms of investment and budgets.

Return on shareholders' capital is typically compared with alternative forms of investment, where the risk is of an equal or similar nature, in order to judge whether the present investment is worth retaining. This is academic for the small business, since the proprietor usually has no alternative to being in business on his or her own account. The ratio

$$\frac{\text{profit after tax} \times 100}{\text{share capital} + \text{reserves}}$$

expresses profit after tax (so that different tax rates on different forms of investment can be taken into account in the comparison) as a percentage of share capital and reserves (the shareholders' interest in the business).

Example:

$$
\begin{array}{cc}
\textit{1988} & \textit{1987} \\
\end{array}
$$

Alcock's $\dfrac{6651 \times 100}{13261} = 50.1\%$ $\qquad$ $\dfrac{3256 \times 100}{6610} = 49.2\%$

SCS $\dfrac{11254 \times 100}{26911} = 41.8\%$ $\qquad$ $\dfrac{1787 \times 100}{15657} = 11.4\%$

Alcock's showed a small improvement in profitability over the two years (from 49.2 per cent to 50.1 per cent), whereas SCS jumped from 11.4 per cent to 41.8 per cent. The owners of Alcock's would not be disappointed with their performance; SCS has improved markedly over the period. We cannot compare the two businesses, as they are in quite different industries and we know nothing else about them. Furthermore, it is not possible to say whether the returns are particularly high, as they are sensitive to owners' remuneration. Net profit can be readily adjusted downwards simply by taking out a higher salary. We would also have to know something about the average returns in the industry to make a valid judgement.

Return on net assets measures the return on total investment or capital employed in the business and is a valuable addition to the return on shareholders' capital, as it takes into account capital raised from other than equity sources. The ratio

$$\frac{\text{profit before interest and tax} \times 100}{\text{capital employed}}$$

expresses profit before finance and tax charges in order to compare businesses with different capital structures and tax liabilities as a percentage of capital employed (shareholders' interest plus long-term borrowings).

Example:

	1988	*1987*
Alcock's	$\dfrac{10884 \times 100}{19375} = 56.1\%$	$\dfrac{6867 \times 100}{14524} = 47.2\%$
SCS	$\dfrac{24514 \times 100}{43281} = 56.6\%$	$\dfrac{6503 \times 100}{26738} = 24.3\%$

Both companies showed an increase in return on total capital employed, which demonstrates that they used their assets more profitably over the period.

Gross profit margin measures the relationship between fixed and variable costs, and sales. It is vitally important as a measure of the intensity of competition, pricing policy, product mix, marketing strategy, production efficiency and purchasing efficiency. These factors alone are likely to determine the success or failure of the business. Gross profit (see the profit and loss account earlier) represents contribution to overhead costs after materials and other production costs have been accounted for and is expressed as a percentage of sales:

$$\frac{\text{gross profit} \times 100}{\text{sales}}$$

where gross profit = sales − cost of sales.

Gross profit margin will tend to stabilize under the following circumstances:

1 where competition is less intense, so that prices in general do not come under pressure;
2 where pricing policy seeks to maintain margins by allowing for discounts, wastage, negotiations on prices and other decisions which affect prices;
3 where individual margins on the mix of products sold achieve the average required for the business as a whole;
4 where individual margins in different customer segments achieve the average required for the business as a whole;
5 where production costs, including materials, direct labour and other factory overheads, are contained within their expected relationship to output;
6 where the cost of materials and stock is held to budgeted levels.

Example:

	1988	*1987*
Alcock's	$\dfrac{64790 \times 100}{154670} = 41.8\%$	$\dfrac{58343 \times 100}{132898} = 43.9\%$
SCS	$\dfrac{149345 \times 100}{225626} = 66.1\%$	$\dfrac{85713 \times 100}{147158} = 58.2\%$

Alcock's experienced a small decline in gross profit margin (43.9 per cent to 41.8 per cent) as a result of one of the factors mentioned above. In contrast, SCS experienced a healthy rise in gross profit margin (from 58.2 per cent to 66.1 per cent). It would require a closer examination of the company's operations and policies before a conclusion could be reached about the causes of the changes.

Net profit margin expresses net profit as a proportion of sales income. Net profit is arrived at after deducting all regular expenses from sales income. Only extraordinary items and tax are still to be deducted. (Tax is not an expense but rather a charge on profit.) Net profit is important because, as the ultimate measure of profitability, it is usually the first financial objective of a company and its comparability over time and between companies in the same industry makes it an ideal yardstick against which performance can be measured. Net profit margin is represented by

$$\frac{\text{net profit before tax} \times 100}{\text{sales income}}$$

where profit before tax is normally also before extraordinary charges. The difference between net and gross profit is overhead expenditure (fixed costs) and any significant changes in selling, administrative and finance expenses will be revealed in net profit margins.

Example:

	1988	1987
Alcock's	$\dfrac{9096 \times 100}{154670} = 5.8\%$	$\dfrac{5087 \times 100}{132898} = 3.8\%$
SCS	$\dfrac{18011 \times 100}{225626} = 7.9\%$	$\dfrac{2849 \times 100}{147158} = 1.9\%$

Both companies have experienced increases in net profit margins. Alcock's showed a considerable improvement with net profit up by 78.8 per cent (£5087 to £9096) when sales growth was only 16.3 per cent and gross profit increased by only 11.0 per cent. Much of the increase in net profit has resulted from a tightening up of overhead expenditure.

SCS also experienced very rapid growth in net profit (up six times) after sales income grew by 53.3 per cent and gross profit by 74.2 per cent. Much of the increase in net profit resulted from improved gross margins and not from lower overheads.

In order to explain changes in overhead expenditure and its effects on net profit margin, there are a number of overhead expenditure ratios which reveal where the main changes have occurred. The inventive financial analyst could produce ratios of almost anything in the business, but we shall restrict the overhead ratios to cover the main expenditure areas of selling and distribution, administration (in particular rent, rates and salaries) and finance.

Selling and distribution expenses (like gross and net profit) can be related to sales income

$$\frac{\text{selling and distribution expenses} \times 100}{\text{sales income}}$$

to produce a marketing costs to sales ratio. This will be helpful in controlling marketing costs and evaluating the success of different combinations of marketing expenditure.

Example:

	1988	*1987*
Alcock's	$\dfrac{10871 \times 100}{154670} = 7.0\%$	$\dfrac{10288 \times 100}{132898} = 7.7\%$
SCS	$\dfrac{23850 \times 100}{225626} = 10.5\%$	$\dfrac{15354 \times 100}{147158} = 10.4\%$

Alcock's spent proportionately more on marketing in 1987 (though only fractionally so) whereas SCS slightly increased its proportion in 1988. In other words, each £1 of marketing expenditure produced £9.46 of sales in 1988 but £9.58 of sales in 1987. These changes are not significant in terms of overall performance of the business and do not therefore explain the variations in performance.

Administration expenses can be treated in the same way to assess their contribution to changes in net profit. Within this grouping of expenses, the largest contributors are premises costs (rent and rates) and salary costs (salaries and directors' remuneration), which require separate treatment. This would be the same for most businesses, although there could be other major cost areas within administration expenses which would justify separate treatment.

Taking each of these in turn, expenses are expressed as a percentage of sales income:

$$\frac{\text{administration expenses} \times 100}{\text{sales income}}$$

Example:

	1988	*1987*
Alcock's	$\dfrac{38395 \times 100}{154670} = 24.8\%$	$\dfrac{36718 \times 100}{132898} = 27.6\%$
SCS	$\dfrac{87965 \times 100}{225626} = 38.9\%$	$\dfrac{57331 \times 100}{147158} = 38.9\%$

Alcock's experienced a small decline in administration expenses as a proportion of sales, whereas SCS was constant.

$$\frac{(\text{rent} + \text{rates}) \times 100}{\text{sales income}}$$

Example:

	1988	*1987*
Alcock's	$\dfrac{10500 \times 100}{154670} = 6.8\%$	$\dfrac{10500 \times 100}{132898} = 7.9\%$
SCS	$\dfrac{8712 \times 100}{225626} = 3.8\%$	$\dfrac{6307 \times 100}{147158} = 4.2\%$

The ratios reveal that each company managed to squeeze a little more sales income from its premises, which suggests that administration has become more efficient (or that the working area is a little cramped!).

$$\frac{\text{overhead salaries} + \text{directors' remuneration} \times 100}{\text{sales income}}$$

Example:

	1988		*1987*	
Alcock's	$\dfrac{20560 \times 100}{154670}$	$= 13.2\%$	$\dfrac{19760 \times 100}{132898}$	$= 14.8\%$
SCS	$\dfrac{61998 \times 100}{225626}$	$= 27.4\%$	$\dfrac{39260 \times 100}{147158}$	$= 26.6\%$

Alcock's improved (slightly) its overhead salaries ratio; SCS saw a marginal decline. It appears that neither company experienced a significant change in overheads and, within the broad grouping, there was nothing worth remarking on. We could conclude that administration costs have been well controlled. In other words, in Alcock's Joinery each £1 spent on administration produced £3.84 worth of sales in 1988, up from £3.61 in 1987. In SCS, the equivalent position was £2.56 in both years, a higher administration cost per unit of sale than Alcock's Joinery.

Finance expenses (like the other expenditure categories above) are related to sales income

$$\frac{\text{finance expenses} \times 100}{\text{sales income}}$$

to produce a finance costs to sales ratio. This will be helpful in evaluating the success of different combinations of finance.

Example:

	1988		*1987*	
Alcock's	$\dfrac{1788 \times 100}{154670}$	$= 1.1\%$	$\dfrac{1780 \times 100}{132898}$	$= 1.3\%$
SCS	$\dfrac{6503 \times 100}{225626}$	$= 2.8\%$	$\dfrac{3654 \times 100}{147158}$	$= 2.4\%$

Neither company endured a high level of financial charges and the proportions were too insignificant to affect performance.

Financial status ratios

Financial stability is an important objective of business planning from the point of view of flexibility in meeting immediate and future liabilities. The level of profit is one measure of long-term viability; thus gross and net profit margin are helpful in assessing whether the business is likely to generate sufficient cash to meet its future obligations. But we also require measures of short-term liquidity, as an indication of the firm's ability to meet its immediate obligations to creditors. There are three basic ratios of financial status which reflect the firm's short-term position.

The current ratio measures the firm's ability to meet its short-term creditors (trade suppliers, VAT, PAYE, taxation, the overdraft) from short-term receivables (current assets such as debtors, stock and cash). It is a simple ratio based on the excess of current assets over current liabilities

$$\frac{\text{current assets}}{\text{current liabilities}}$$

and is particularly useful to creditors as an early warning of a borrower's impending cash crisis. As long as current assets exceed current liabilities (which means that the ratio is above unity), there must be more than £1 of the former to meet each £1 of the latter. This suggests a degree of short-term financial stability.

Example:

	1988	*1987*
Alcock's	$\frac{24134}{19328} = 1.24$	$\frac{15933}{14543} = 1.09$
SCS	$\frac{69051}{58236} = 1.18$	$\frac{34240}{30133} = 1.13$

Both companies improved their short-term liquidity over the period, with Alcock's showing the better performance. Without knowing what typical current ratios obtain in their respective industries, it is not possible to say whether these ratios are relatively good or bad. With each £1 of liabilities covered by £1.24 (Alcock's) and £1.18 (SCS), however, it appears that neither company had any trouble paying its short-term debts.

The acid test extends the measure of liquidity a little further by excluding from the calculation stock and work in progress. They are considered, on a conservative basis, to be relatively 'illiquid' for the purposes of the acid test, which takes into account only debtors and cash

$$\frac{\text{debtors} + \text{cash}}{\text{current liabilities}}$$

and indicates how readily the company can meet its short-term liabilities. The acid test is so called because it is the ultimate test of liquidity.

Example:

	1988		*1987*
Alcock's	$\dfrac{20344}{19328} = 1.05$		$\dfrac{13803}{14543} = 0.94$
SCS	$\dfrac{57776}{58236} = 0.99$		$\dfrac{29110}{30133} = 0.96$

The ratios are lower than the current ratios because stock and work in progress have been excluded. Alcock's still managed to cover its current liabilities in 1988 (£1 current liabilities covered by £1.05 current assets) with SCS just short of complete cover (£1 current liabilities covered by £0.99 current assets). While it would be ideal to show an acid test of more than 1, it is acceptable to show cover as close as possible to 1. On these grounds, both companies had adequate cover over the past two years.

The debt or gearing ratio discloses how highly borrowed (geared) the company is at the end of the year, by expressing long-term borrowings (of two years or more) as a proportion of total capital employed, including loans and shareholders' interest:

$$\frac{\text{long-term loans} \times 100}{\text{capital employed}}$$

The importance of the gearing ratio lies in determining whether the company is in a position to borrow more to meet its longer-term needs, particularly on occasions when the liquidity ratios (current ratio and acid test) demonstrate that additional borrowing might be required to meet short-term needs also. This typically happens when the overdraft develops a 'hard core' of permanent borrowing and should ideally (from both the lender's and borrower's points of view) be transferred into a loan over a term of years.

There may be other reasons for raising additional loan capital (such as when new equipment or vehicles are needed) and the gearing ratio would reveal whether the company was under- or over-borrowed. A ratio of around 50 per cent reveals that for every £1 of borrowed money there is £2 of total capital (in other words, £1 of the bank's money to £1 of the company's), whereas gearing of 67 per cent reveals £2 of borrowed money to £3 of total capital employed. The ideal gearing level depends very much on the purpose for which the money has been borrowed: the purchase of property could bear a higher gearing ratio than the purchase of a vehicle, because the former is a more solid asset from the lender's point of view and therefore has a more certain market value in the event of the debtor's being unable to meet its commitments.

Example:

	1988	1987

$$\text{Alcock's } \frac{6114 \times 100}{19375} = 31.5\% \qquad \frac{7914 \times 100}{14524} = 54.4\%$$

$$\text{SCS } \frac{16370 \times 100}{43281} = 37.8 \qquad \frac{11081 \times 100}{26738} = 41.4\%$$

Alcock's reduced its gearing to a more acceptable level by repaying part of the bank loan over the year (which affects the numerator and denominator) and increasing profit (which affects the denominator). At this point it could borrow more if it wished to do so, since the gearing ratio is relatively low.

SCS also reduced its gearing a little, largely by increasing profit, although hire-purchase facilities increased over the period. SCS could also increase its gearing as at present it appears to be under-borrowed.

Financial management ratios

The efficient management of capital in the business is an important indicator of performance, in that inefficient management tends to tie up capital unnecessarily, which is expensive in terms of interest charges and a constraint on borrowing additional capital for short- and long-term purposes. In short, if capital already available in the business could be better utilized, additional borrowing would be largely unnecessary or would be available on more favourable terms (since there would be more unencumbered assets available to support bank borrowing). We are concerned here principally with the management of working capital: stock, debtors and creditors.

Stock days measures how many days stock and work in progress the business requires in order to satisfy a given level of sales. Optimum stock levels can be calculated for each product line by relating stock to purchases required for anticipated sales for the coming period and the order and delivery lead times from suppliers:

$$\frac{\text{stock} \times 365}{\text{purchases}}$$

Thus there would be an ideal stock holding level (closing stock) expressed in number of days and related to purchases in the period (or to sales, if purchases are not available).

Example:

	1988	*1987*
Alcock's	$\dfrac{3790 \times 365}{35290} = 39$ days	$\dfrac{2130 \times 365}{31045} = 25$ days
SCS	$\dfrac{11275 \times 365}{82426} = 50$ days	$\dfrac{5130 \times 365}{56905} = 33$ days

Both companies increased their stock and work in progress quite considerably over the period. Alcock's Joinery would not normally need high stock levels as most wood products and consumables would be available from local wholesalers at short notice, and so a level of 39 days seems a little high. SCS probably required higher levels of work in progress (up from 33 to 50 days) to account for the writing of specially tailored computer programs still to be invoiced. (There is the danger of assuming that the ratios apply uniformly throughout the period, whereas they are calculated on the end of year figures only. This should be borne in mind when analysing financial accounts, as it is quite possible for exceptional circumstances to prevail at the end of year, which could invalidate many of the conclusions drawn about the financial management and stability of the companies.)

Debtor days measures the number of days taken by customers to pay their bills and is calculated by expressing the amount of debtors at the year end in relation to sales income:

$$\frac{\text{debtors} \times 365}{\text{sales income}}$$

The ideal number of debtor days would depend on the terms of trade in the industry concerned. Where terms are for payment within 30 days of the date of invoice, we would expect average debtors to be about 45 days, allowing for postal delays and the accounting schedules of customers (it would be very inefficient to pay every bill exactly when it was due). Where 60 days are the norm, we would expect average debtors to be about 75 days, allowing for delays. In times of high interest rates and reduced profitability, we would expect debtors to extend beyond the 45 to 75 day range, and in industries where even longer payment terms are the norm, it would not be surprising to find debtors of over 100 days.

Example:

	1988	*1987*
Alcock's	$\dfrac{16863 \times 365}{154670} = 40$ days	$\dfrac{13203 \times 365}{132898} = 36$ days
SCS	$\dfrac{46361 \times 365}{225626} = 75$ days	$\dfrac{29028 \times 365}{147158} = 72$ days

The companies exhibited quite different debtor periods: Alcock's was 40 days and SCS's was 75 days. Since some of Alcock's work was for private customers who would have paid cash on completion, it is not surprising that debtor days were relatively low. SCS's customers, in contrast, were taking nearly three months to pay their bills. In order to reach a firm conclusion about the reason for the lengthening of both companies' debtor days, we would have to enquire of the companies what their terms of trade were and how they exercised control over credit given to customers. Credit control is discussed in chapter 5.

Creditor days measures the number of days taken by the company to pay its suppliers (to include trade suppliers only) and is calculated by expressing the amount of creditors at the year end in relation to purchases (or to sales income where purchases are not available):

$$\frac{\text{creditors} \times 365}{\text{purchases}}$$

The number of creditor days would depend on the terms of trade offered by the supplier. In order to maintain good relations with suppliers (buying and selling are reciprocal activities and both parties should stand to gain in a healthy and mutually beneficial relationship), it would be sensible business practice to pay bills when they fall due, allowing for your own payment schedules (it is good practice to get into the habit of paying accounts on the same day each month). Thus, if the terms set by your suppliers are 30 days from date of invoice, you will have about 45 creditor days, given the delays and typical end of month payment schedules.

Example:

	1988	*1987*
Alcock's	$\dfrac{6285 \times 365}{35290} = 65$ days	$\dfrac{5188 \times 365}{31045} = 61$ days
SCS	$\dfrac{12420 \times 365}{82426} = 55$ days	$\dfrac{9198 \times 365}{56905} = 59$ days

Both companies took about two months to pay their suppliers, which suggests that they were taking longer credit than was strictly due. Alcock's took even longer in 1988 (from 61 to 65 days), whereas SCS shortened its creditor days from 59 to 55.

Resource management ratios

Apart from financial resources, a business has to look after its other physical resources, such as its employees, premises and equipment. Efficient management of these resources is an important indicator of performance, since people and fixed assets contribute to the work effort required to generate sales and produce and to deliver output. Their measurement is just as important as the other assets described earlier.

Sales per employee measures the amount of sales income generated on average by each member of the workforce and is expressed in terms of

$$\frac{\text{sales income}}{\text{no. of employees}}$$

where number of employees includes all full- and part-time production, sales and administrative staff, as well as directors working in the business. Sales per employee is a simple measure of progress when compared year-on-year and can be compared with other firms in the industry as an indicator of efficiency in utilizing available capacity. In our examples, Alcock's had seven employees in 1988 and six in 1987; SCS had five in 1988 and four in 1987 (the directors were non-executive).

Example:

	1988	*1987*
Alcock's	$\dfrac{£154670}{7} = £22095$	$\dfrac{£132898}{6} = £22149$
SCS	$\dfrac{£225626}{5} = £45125$	$\dfrac{£147158}{4} = £36789$

Alcock's showed no improvement at all in sales per employee; SCS advanced from £36789 to £45125, an increase of 22 per cent. Once again, it is not possible to conclude that Alcock's performed poorly and SCS well, since we know nothing about the available capacity of the firm. For instance, Alcock's could be at full stretch (and so would show very little gain in sales per employee), while SCS could be operating below full capacity (and so could easily register an increase in sales per employee).

Profit per employee measures the amount of net profit before tax generated on average by each member of the workforce:

$$\frac{\text{net profit before tax}}{\text{no. of employees}}$$

Like sales per employee, profit per employee measures progress when compared year-on-year and can be compared with other firms in the industry as an indicator of the profitability of utilizing available capacity.

Example:

	1988	*1987*
Alcock's	$\dfrac{£9096}{7} = £1299$	$\dfrac{£5087}{6} = £847$
SCS	$\dfrac{£18011}{5} = £3602$	$\dfrac{£2849}{4} = £712$

Alcock's showed a respectable improvement in profit per employee, whereas SCS made exceptional gains. Both companies performed well in respect of profit generated per employee.

Productivity gains are measured in terms of changes in gross profit per productive employee over the year, which is a more appropriate measure of performance of the productive workforce (those who are engaged in making or delivering output for customers) than net profit per employee (which measures both productive and non-productive workers) and is relevant only to manufacturing businesses. The equation

$$\frac{\text{gross profit}}{\text{no. of productive employees}}$$

requires accurate knowledge of the number of productive workers. In our two examples, only Alcock's had productive employees:

$$\text{Alcock's } \quad \frac{\pounds 64790}{5} = \pounds 12958 \qquad \frac{\pounds 58343}{4} = \pounds 14585$$

1988	1987

Productivity per employee dropped over the year. Although gross profit rose by 11 per cent (from £58343 to £64790), direct labour rose by 25 per cent (from four people to five), the net result of which was a decline in gross profit per employee of 11.1 per cent. This outcome would normally accompany an expansion where the new workers were not yet fully productive and is not necessarily due to poor management of resources.

Investment efficiency is our final ratio, although not at all of least importance. The equation

$$\frac{\text{sales turnover}}{\text{fixed assets}}$$

measures the efficiency of use of the fixed assets (or investment) in terms of the level of sales generated by each £1 spent on plant, equipment, machinery, vehicles, buildings and intangible assets. (Fixed assets are measured net of depreciation.) This is an important ratio as expenditure on fixed assets represents a major decision variable in the business – commitment to expansion, for instance, requires the purchase of additional equipment which, in order to earn its way, has to generate an acceptable level of sales.

Example:

$$\text{Alcock's } \quad \frac{\pounds 154670}{\pounds 14569} = \pounds 10.61 \qquad \frac{\pounds 132898}{\pounds 13134} = \pounds 10.11$$

$$\text{SCS } \quad \frac{\pounds 225626}{\pounds 32466} = \pounds 6.94 \qquad \frac{\pounds 147158}{\pounds 22631} = \pounds 6.50$$

Neither business showed a startling improvement in its utilization of fixed assets. Alcock's improved utilization efficiency by 4.9 per cent and SCS by 6.7 per cent. In other words, each £1 spent on fixed assets in 1988 generated sales of £10.61 (Alcock's) and £6.94 (SCS). It would not be fair to form a view of the relative performance of the companies, as we would need to know rather more about them first (such as how many years they had been in business and how old their equipment was).

In summary, Alcock's Joinery saw only a modest increase in sales income to £154670 (up 11 per cent over the period) but lifted net profit by 78.8 per cent to £9096, despite a small decline in gross profit margin (from 43.9 per cent to 41.8 per cent). The improvement was largely due to control of fixed overheads and in particular administration costs, which declined as a proportion of sales from 27.6 per cent to 24.8 per cent. Return on shareholders' funds was almost static at 50 per cent. The company's financial status improved over the period, with small gains in working capital and liquidity and a decline in overall gearing. Management of financial and other resources saw mixed results, with stock days lengthening from 25 to 39 days and debtors out to 40 days, although a small amount of additional credit was taken from suppliers to balance the increase in current assets. Sales per employee was static at £22000 but profit per employee improved from £800 to over £1300. Turning to finance, additional fixed capital and working capital requirements were minimal and were more than adequately covered by an increase in long-term funds (profit) and short-term bank borrowing (the overdraft). At the year ending 31 March 1988, the company appeared to be financially sound.

SCS experienced rapid growth in sales income to £225626 (up 53% over the period) and lifted net profit 6 times to £18011. The considerable improvement was largely due to a jump of 74 per cent in gross profit, up from 58 per cent to 66 per cent as a proportion of sales. Fixed overheads remained constant as a proportion of sales over the period. Return on shareholders' funds rose from 11 per cent to 42 per cent. The company's financial status improved marginally over the period, with small gains in working capital and liquidity and a small decline in overall gearing to 37 per cent. Financial management ratios were mixed, with stock days lengthening from 33 to 50 days and debtors out to 75 days. Sales per employee increased from £36000 to £45000 and profit per employee improved from £700 to over £3600. Turning to finance, growth in fixed capital (additional investment in equipment and vehicles) and working capital (stock and debtors) was quite considerable and was financed by an increase in long-term funds (profit and hire-purchase facilities) and short-term bank borrowing (the overdraft). At the year ending 31 March 1988, the company appeared to be financially sound.

The only way to understand the use of ratios is to apply them to your own business over a period of several years. Start with the last two years' accounts and calculate the above ratios in the way we have done. What do your own performance measures tell you?

Key points

- Current performance is normally measured against both budgets and previous years' accounts.
- The most important measures of profitability are gross profit to sales, which demonstrates marketing effectiveness, and net profit to sales, which (additionally) demonstrates how overheads have been controlled.
- Being able to meet short-term debts is at the heart of financial stability and short-term liquidity ratios are a useful measure of imminent problems.
- Tying up capital unnecessarily in stock and debtors is costly and cash flow problems can often be alleviated by tightening up controls in these areas.
- Asset utilization (people as well as plant and equipment) is just as important as making profit, so improving the utilization of assets can result in substantial benefits.

4

Forecasting and budgeting procedures

> **Outline**
>
> A successful business is dependent on good planning. This chapter describes:
>
> - corporate planning
> - the two main forecasting methods used in small businesses
> - how to prepare a sales forecast
> - how to do budgeted monthly profit and loss accounts
> - cashflow forecasting
> - balance sheet forecasting

Most people in business are reluctant to look ahead more than a few days or weeks, particularly if they have short order books. There is no virtue in looking too far ahead, yet there is a need to plan for the immediate future. It is to this future that we now turn: in this chapter we shall examine the forward planning process (and write a short corporate plan for Alcock's) and review forecasting methods and budgeting techniques. We shall project profit and loss accounts, balance sheets and cash flow forecasts and produce monthly budgets. The aim is to enable you to produce your own forecasts and budgets for the coming year.

The greater the degree of uncertainty, the more pressing the need to plan and forecast, since the prime objective of the planning and forecasting process is to *identify future requirements and attempt to have some influence over future events*. The attraction of forecasting lies in the way that it attempts to represent in simple financial terms management's endeavours to shape the future in order to take maximum advantage of available opportunities, mobilize capacity to deliver on the opportunities and ensure that the business is adequately financed to maximize returns.

Planning and forecasting allow managers to prepare the ground for exploitation, rather than risk all in the hope that fortune will favour the adventurous. There are many instances where bold and daring initiatives *have* paid off handsomely but there are even more where abject failure has been the outcome. Being the gambler certainly has its glamorous side, particularly when risks are high and the prize is brought home.

In other words, planning and forecasting are not without their limitations and it takes an experienced business planner and forecaster to prepare the ground for maximum gain from business activity. The road to successful planning and forecasting lies in careful and considered analysis of the historical facts, together with a judicious interpretation of future trends and the capabilities of the business in question. There is more science than art to forecasting, although even the most experienced business forecasters admit to a small degree of good fortune when their forecasts turn out to be more than 90 per cent accurate.

Planning is the general term for the activity that encompasses both forecasting and budgeting. Although we shall necessarily need to touch on business planning in this section, we shall not be dealing with it in any great depth. The directors will require detailed business plans setting out where the business is going (objectives), how it intends to achieve its objectives by competing in the marketplace (strategy and forecasts), how it intends to implement the strategy (detailed action plans and budgets) and how it is to be financed. The forecasts and budgets are simply a financial representation of the written business plans.

It is not possible to say which comes first: plans or forecasts. There is one school of thought which prefers to see written plans based on what the business owners want to achieve, with broad financial forecasts and detailed budgets supporting these plans. Another school says that forecasts are the first stage of the planning process in the mature business, within which detailed plans and budgets must be made to fit. Ultimately, however, plans and forecasts are part of the same iterative process: planning and forecasting require continuous development by means of moving backwards and forwards between actions, ideas and the revenues and costs associated with them, until a balance is achieved. In other words, the plans should be achievable and the forecasts realistic.

The corporate plan: setting objectives and strategies

The question of planning for future growth is one of 'to what degree should planning be *formalized* in the business?' All businesses have implicit plans, even if they are only a mental commitment to a course of action or amount merely to putting together cash flow forecasts for the bank manager. There are therefore different types of plans and different levels of planning activity. There is the *business or financing plan* which is used to raise finance from external sources; there is the *corporate plan* for internal use which is used to identify strategies, plans and financial outcomes; there are *marketing plans* to identify sales and marketing needs; there are various operations and staffing plans for internal use in the business. We are concerned here with the corporate plan, which is the internal planning document. (Financing plans will be dealt with in chapter 6.)

The functional activities (marketing, recruitment, production etc.) across various divisional activities (selling into different markets) in a business give rise either to revenues and associated costs, or just to costs, and are reflected financially in the profit and loss account. Corporate or strategic planning examines the way in which a company integrates its business divisions and its functions to produce an overall effect and therefore its importance lies in seeking to explain *where profits come from* at the end of the day. Corporate planning need not be very formal. Indeed, almost all businesses are actually pursuing strategies, though many small ones would not recognize the fact. Since they all tend to abandon unprofitable, or marginal, business activities, they are implicitly attempting to concentrate on what they are good at (their strengths), while recognizing their weaknesses and trying to reduce their impact. This is the basis of strategic planning.

The functions of a written corporate plan are diverse:

1 promotion of teamwork amongst staff, managers and directors by involving them in the planning process, particularly in identifying and analysing internal strengths and weaknesses;
2 integration of various divisions and functions into a strategic and coherent whole through careful and considered analysis of each component of the business;

3 identification of resources required to implement the strategy, particularly physical and human resources;
4 identification of potential problems and opportunities and actions required to meet them;
5 acting as a control device by measuring outcomes against plans and forecasts.

Planning is best done by the directors of the company, possibly with assistance from professional advisers. There is considerable value in the directors undertaking the planning themselves because of the knowledge gained in the process of trying to understand what makes the business succeed and how profit arises.

The starting point for the corporate planning process is to decide on the longer-term objectives of the business and the strategy and action plans required to achieve these objectives. Once this has been done, further analysis of the company's strengths and weaknesses can be undertaken and the forecasts produced.

(1) *Setting company objectives* for the overall planning period, as well as for each individual trading year. The period chosen is a matter of the individual company's preferences, trading conditions in the industry and lead times required to launch new activities successfully in the marketplace. Fundamentally, the business owners must feel comfortable with the planning period, otherwise they will lack confidence in the plan. Typically, smaller companies should be planning over a two to three year period, unless they require longer lead times for marketing activity to impact on sales.

Objectives should be achievable and, as far as possible, measurable. There are no rules as to what is a legitimate objective, but there are some guidelines to bear in mind when setting objectives. It is sensible to divide objectives into the following categories:

(a) *personal objectives*, which should reflect the personal needs of the owners in the short and longer terms. Some common personal objectives are the desired growth rate (consolidation rather than growth is very much a personal matter), reduction of hours spent in the office (always a thorny issue for the owners), raising directors' salary levels (the owners may feel that they have been subsidizing the business for long enough), introduction of family or other partners into ownership and management positions (the question of succession could arise), and sale of all or part of the business (frequently the owners want to exit).

(b) *business objectives*, which are generally of a financial or non-financial nature. Examples of the former include net profit on sales (a prime objective in all businesses, whatever their size), profit growth, sales growth, return on investment, growth in net assets and growth in net worth. The latter include a wide range of marketing, organizational, managerial, employment, legal and other objectives, often subordinate to the prime financial ones. Not all of these need be quantifiable, as long as they serve a purpose. For instance, a legitimate objective would be to provide congenial working conditions and employ the most contented workforce in the industry. These objectives would be hard to measure, but they might play a vital role in developing a positive working environment, which itself could have measurable consequences for employee productivity.

(2) *Identifying and analysing the basis for a strategy* follows the objectives and starts with what is commonly called a *SWOT analysis*, an acronym for strengths, weaknesses, opportunities and threats. SWOT is a way of analysing the *entire* business from top to bottom, inside and outside, in order to establish precisely what aspects of the internal operation and the external environment should form the basis of future growth. The analysis can readily be undertaken by the owner but it is preferable to involve other directors, managers and staff, for the simple reason that one person's view could be distorted (and quite naturally often is, since we all have different ways of perceiving things about us) and therefore would not represent the true SWOT facing the business. The SWOT analysis starts with an examination of internal strengths and weaknesses and their significance to the business, and goes on to examine opportunities and threats and their probability of happening.

(a) *Strengths and weaknesses* are the starting point. To begin, it is worth producing a 'checklist' of all the conceivable internal facets of the business and thinking very carefully about their strengths and weaknesses in turn:

> *products*
> quality of products and services

features of products and services
product research and development

production
quality of plant, equipment, premises
production methods
technology of production
production staff
production management
sources of supply

marketing
customer base
pricing policies
promotional activities
sales and distribution staffing and activities
research
sales and marketing management

finance
capitalization
gearing
profitability
control systems
financial management

management and organization
quality of owners/directors
quality of managers
soundness of structure
culture and morale
quality of administration
attitudes and loyalty of staff

Not only is it worth getting other people in the company to do the exercise, but on the marketing side there is every reason to find out direct from your customers (present as well as past) what they think. Having written out a list of strengths and weaknesses under each of the above points and had them corroborated by customers and staff, consider their relative significance and eliminate those items which are of least importance. You should be left with a handful of meaningful points which should shape the basis on which the strategy is to be built.

(b) *Opportunities and threats* cover the external factors affecting the operations of the business. Another checklist helps to identify areas in the external environment from which opportunities or threats could emerge:

> *competition*
> changes in strategies of existing competitors
> emergence of new competitors
>
> *political factors*
> new government (local/national/abroad)
> new policies
> new legislation
>
> *economic factors*
> structural change
> cyclical change
> inflation
> exchange rates
> international factors
>
> *social factors*
> demographic change
> cultural and social change
>
> *technological factors*
> improvements in technology

A listing of strengths and weaknesses should lead to a short internal debate about the probabilities of their becoming reality. In this case, it would be wise to consult outsiders about their views, and regular monitoring of major economic and political changes would help to inform the listing process. Change is inevitable, and so this part of the analysis is vital.

(3) *Setting out and evaluating the components of a strategy* follows logically from the SWOT analysis. The choices facing the directors have already been considerably reduced by means of the SWOT analysis and by sorting and listing the strengths, weaknesses, opportunities and threats. Strategy should build on strengths (while

overcoming weaknesses), taking into account areas of major opportunity and the threats revealed in the external environment. From these listings, a final set of strategic choices for the period emerges:

choice of products or services offered

production choices, including equipment and premises

customer and marketing choices

organizational, management and staffing choices

financial requirements and choice of financing methods

In the aggregate, these choices will amount to a strategy which should be selected and evaluated on the basis of consistency and realism in the light of the SWOT analysis, the impact of proposed changes and the acceptability of the strategy to the people who work in the business. Questions to ask yourself are as follows:

(a) Are the choices mutually compatible? In other words, will the product range suit the chosen market and can sales be delivered with available capacity?

(b) Are the choices consistent with corporate strengths and weaknesses? A strategy should exploit strengths, not weaknesses.

(c) Are the choices compatible with corporate objectives? Given the choices made, can the business achieve its stated objectives in the period?

(d) Is there internal harmony and is efficiency maintained? The choices must not be allowed to disrupt (for long) the smooth working of existing activities.

(e) Is there compatibility between products and markets? Research will need to show that new customer segments have demonstrated a need for the proposed product range.

(f) Can the choices be accommodated within the existing resource base? What other resources will be needed?

(g) Is there sufficient cash to fund short-term needs? Is longer-term profitability assured? It is surprising how many businesses proceed with a course of action without knowing whether it will be profitable.

At this point, the strategy should emerge naturally from the choices identified earlier. A strategy is a way of competing in the marketplace for a share of sales, based on what the business is good at (its strengths) and the opportunities identified through research or experience. A statement of strategy should be brief and unambiguous, encapsulating the essential choices made earlier. A change in strategy implies that the original choice was wrong (and therefore the planning process needs careful review) or that circumstances have changed significantly (the SWOT attributes have been replaced by an entirely new set). As an example of a corporate plan, we produce one for Alcock's Joinery in the appendix (the figures will be produced later).

(4) *Producing forecasts and budgets* over the planning period for the chosen strategy completes the planning process. Forecasting is the process of representing in financial terms the likely outcomes of a given course of action. Forecasting financial outcomes means producing projected *profit and loss accounts, balance sheets and cash flows* for a given period, normally in outline form only, rather than in complete detail. Forecasts give a general picture for a period of several years ahead, rather than pointing to specific detail. They differ from budgets in this respect. Budgets are generally for a shorter period (typically one year) and provide considerable detail of revenues and expenditure. They relate very closely to working plans and are also used as a basis for monitoring actual sales revenue and expenditure. (We return to the use of budgets as a control device in chapter 5.) We start by looking closely at the forecasting process and turn later to budgeting procedures.

Forecasting methods

There are two main forecasting methods. The first builds on historical financial data, taking into account business plans for the coming period, present and future influences on patterns of demand (such as competition and the other external factors mentioned above in the SWOT analysis) and the probable costs of doing business in the future. The second more or less ignores historical information (or gives relatively little weight to it) and is based on achieving sales targets at planned expenditure levels, either at an agreed level of profit or (typically in the first three years) at a break-even level of operation.

The first method would normally be used when the company has been established for several years and has generated sufficient financial data to enable trends in revenues and costs to be identified and relationships between sales and expenditure levels to be calculated (as we did in chapter 3). By definition, trends can only be identified once there is a reasonable history of sales, expenditure and the financing of business activity. A 'reasonable history' is hard to define and will differ among businesses in different industries, but generally should cover at least two years of 'normal' activity beyond the initial setting up period (the first three years). This is because the early years of a business are concerned primarily with building sales at the expense of profit (costs tend to be very high in the first three years), and it would be foolish to base forecasts on what is clearly an abnormal situation (the early development of the business). For instance, marketing costs in relation to sales (discussed in chapter 3) will 'settle down' into a consistent pattern once the owner discovers the optimum marketing approach. In the early years, however, there may be considerable variation in marketing approaches from year to year as the owner experiments with different combinations of the marketing 'mix' and consequently there is likely to be an erratic relationship with sales income.

The second method would be used in quite different circumstances. When the company is in its early years and there is no reliable or consistent history on which to base forecasts, and particularly when the business is new, it is necessary to adopt a different approach to forecasting. Starting with the business plan, which sets out where the company wishes to go and how it intends to get there, pre-determined sales income targets, planned expenditure levels and estimated financial requirements can be set, based on either a break-even operation or a profit-making one (at a given level of profit). This would still entail using your knowledge of financial accounting and relationships between revenues and costs covered in the earlier chapters, except that you would of necessity have to apply observed historical relationships with a great deal of care (since they would have probably changed).

Forecasting the financial statements

The forecasting process starts with sales forecasts and proceeds to projected profit and loss accounts, cash flow forecasts and balance sheets. The forecasting steps are as follows.

(1) *Prepare historical accounts*: preliminary work will include assembling the previous five years' profit and loss accounts and balance sheets, which should be readily available from the audited accounts. (If you have a shorter trading history, then put together as many years as are available.) Since the forecasts will be prepared before the end of the current financial year, for which figures will not yet be available, you should use actual accounts to date (available from the books of account) plus budgeted figures for the remainder of the current year. You may have to arrange the figures in an orderly and consistent way (do not assume that your auditors will have necessarily presented the statements in the way that you require them for forecasting purposes), as we have done for Alcock's Joinery and SCS in chapter 2. At the same time, calculate the financial ratios and percentages (as we did earlier) and present them separately. They are indispensable to the forecasting process.

(2) *Prepare the corporate plan*: in order to forecast the profit and loss accounts and balance sheets, you must have decided your company's corporate objectives and strategy in the first instance. The financial data are then simply a monetary representation of the corporate plan, clothing the strategies in something that can be measured and monitored.

(3) *Agree forecasting assumptions and business policies*: forecasting assumptions must be settled in advance and adhered to throughout the forecasting process. To change them would introduce inconsistencies into the forecasts and disappoint you in the outcomes. Assumptions should be based on the following scenarios and policies:

(a) a 'best guess' scenario, which should reflect extrapolations of past performance, suitably adjusted for current trends, internal constraints and resource availability, market opportunities and threats, other environmental factors and personal aspirations and needs;

(b) a pessimistic scenario, reflecting a zero growth or even a break-even outcome, and possibly justified on the grounds of some external event happening, in order to demonstrate that the business can survive even under the most trying conditions;

(c) business policies to be adopted over the planning period, covering production, marketing, finance and employment. The main business policy changes that could affect forecasting include changes in production arrangements (such as whether production should be contracted out or brought inside), changes in marketing (such as pricing policies, use of external sales channels and agency agreements), changes in financial arrangements (such as the financing of assets on an 'off-balance-sheet' basis) and changes in recruitment and employment policies (such as whether to recruit experienced people or train them from scratch). Changes in these policies could affect the outcomes of forecasting, sometimes quite drastically. For this reason they need to be settled in advance.

Depending on whether you are forecasting manually or using a computer spreadsheet, you may wish to run further 'sensitivities', asking 'what if?' on certain key variables in the forecasting equation. Generally speaking, unless you are absolutely certain about expected outcomes over the forecasting period (such as where you have long-term contracts with customers), it is prudent to forecast using:

(a) modest assumptions about growth in sales and gross profit margins;

(b) realistic to cautious assumptions about increases in costs, particularly fixed overheads (which have a habit of getting out of control) – this does not prevent you from setting more ambitious sales and profit targets, but these must be distinguished from forecasts, which have a different purpose.

(4) *Forecast sales income, gross profit and net profit*: net profit margin (net profit on sales) has already been set in the corporate plan as a principal objective for the planning period, and gross profit margin is an automatic outcome of marketing decisions. Indeed, raising the gross profit margin might be a specific objective in its own right. Once gross and net margins have been agreed, and the sales

forecasts produced, then gross and net profit fall naturally into place.

(5) *Complete forecast profit and loss accounts*: by applying the remaining key percentages at the variable and fixed costs levels, detailed expenditure can be completed. (See chapter 2 for a full explanation of the profit and loss account.) We now have a complete set of profit and loss accounts for the planning period and therefore know what contribution profit is likely to make to total funding.

(6) *Forecast cash flow requirements*: the cash flow forecast is probably the best known of all the financial statements. It reveals the cash position at the bank at any point in time – the bank balance – and is indispensable to survival in the short term and particularly to keeping the bank manager happy. The cash flow forecast, as the name suggests, is a monthly forecast (usually for 12 months) of *every type of cash banked* (whether from sales, grants, loans etc.) and *every type of payment* (to suppliers, staff, landlords, banks, advisers, Inland Revenue, Customs and Excise etc.), and by deducting the latter (cash payments) from the former (cash banked) a net flow of cash either into or out of the business is reached for the month. The forecast profit and loss accounts are the source of cash flow forecasts, since they show sales income (from which cash is eventually banked) and expenditure (which leads to payments out of the bank account). Completing the cash flow forecast reveals when the business will need additional *short-term finance* and how much will be needed. In short, it indicates the required overdraft level.

(7) *Forecast balance sheets*: to complete the financial statements, the balance sheets can now be projected in order to show not only what the business will be worth at each year end, but, more importantly, how much additional finance will be needed over the *long term*. The cash flow forecast has shown how much will be required over the short term, but is too detailed a statement for more than 12 months ahead, which renders it impractical as an indicator of longer-term finance. Since the balance sheet also reveals how much finance is being used in the business, it is a useful device for determining future financial needs.

Preparing a sales forecast

A sales forecast sets out the anticipated annual and monthly sales volume (units) and sales revenue (£) to different groups of customers over the planning period. A sales forecast is the starting point for the forecasting process and is required in order to work out the following:

what it will cost to generate sales, or in other words; expenditure associated with sales and marketing decisions;

2 how much work effort will be involved, which will influence scheduling and capacity decisions (in other words, how many people and what plant, equipment and other assets will be needed, and how this will all be organized).

There are three basic methods of sales forecasting:

1 The first is specifically related to new situations (either new businesses or new activities in existing ones) where there is no history and where sales volumes will necessarily be low. The immediate objective is to reach a break-even level of sales as quickly as possible.

2 The second covers situations where there is sufficient information on record about sales volumes and values. Sales forecasts can be built up by projecting sales to individual customers or market groups by product or product group.

3 The third covers businesses where it is not practicable to analyse sales volumes and values by product group and customer segment. Forecasting must rely on extrapolations of past trends, taking into account expected future trends and internal considerations.

Forecasting by volume and value

Sales income is calculated by multiplying the volume of sales (i.e. the number of products or services for sale) by the price charged. Volume will not necessarily be the amount that customers wish to buy. For example, you may wish to produce things in batches of 20, but customers will buy them singly. Forecasting volume therefore requires thinking about customer behaviour, in particular their pattern of buying and the unit of sale that this will involve. This could necessitate some market research. However, there is much to be gained from producing a forecast before you carry out detailed research, as it will help to identify the most important things that you need to find out.

To produce a reliable forecast, you will need to know the following:

1 the volume of sales that can be handled by the existing sales force and, if recruitment is required, how soon new sales capacity can be installed;
2 the break-even sales level, which indicates what level of sales must be achieved in order to survive;
3 the level of demand and in particular customers' buying patterns and preferences.

The best approach is to start with (3), because it is based on customer behaviour, but at certain stages in the development of a business it might be easier to start with (1) or (2), relating this to (3) when market research has been undertaken. Either way, the forecast should proceed through the following stages:

How much can the business sell?
   ↓
Is this enough to create a profitable business?
  ↓   ↓
 YES NO ――――― How can more be sold?
  ↓
Will customers buy this much?
  ↓   ↓
 YES NO ――――― How much will they buy?
  ↓
Does research confirm this?
  ↓   ↓
 YES NO ――――― Back to the drawing board!
  ↓
Complete the forecast

You will probably need to produce several forecasts before being satisfied. As you go through each step, you may well have the choice of altering the volume or the price or both. In addition, there will be a sales history which should provide evidence of sales patterns and growth during past years. You will need to decide whether to take a sober view or whether rapid growth is possible, and all of this should have been settled in the corporate plan. In practice, sensitivities should be run based on different assumptions about sales volumes showing optimistic, pessimistic and 'best guess' scenarios.

The higher the quality of information available at the start, the greater will be the degree of accuracy in the outcomes. To produce reliable forecasts, full details of previous years' sales records will be needed, including sales by volume and value and by product or product range to different groups of customers (market segments). Products and customers can be grouped in many different ways and analysing sales can be a long and arduous task, particularly if sales records are not retained and stored in an easily retrievable form. If you do not attempt a regular analysis of sales records, then now is the time to start! The practice of keeping sales records is dealt with in chapter 5.

The steps in building a forecast are as follows:

1 Identify the unit sale. If your sales vary from customer to customer, you may need to settle on typical or average sales units and you may have to work with more than one type of unit. Each will require a separate forecast.
2 Decide what is a suitable time period for your business. It is unlikely that you will wish to produce a detailed sales forecast for more than 12 months, although you should produce an aggregate annual forecast for the remainder of the planning period (three to five years).
3 Using historical data estimate the number of unit sales in each time period to produce a sales pattern. Now convert this to a monthly volume forecast for each type of unit. Remember to start from a low base and build up sales volumes slowly if the activity is new, since sales are usually hard to make in new markets when products are not widely known.
4 Multiply the volume for each type of unit by the price for that unit to obtain the financial value. Add these values together to give the monthly sales revenue. Sales figures should be rounded to the nearest £1000 to make the arithmetic easier.
5 Compare this figure with your forecast costs. Depending on

whether you are projecting a profit or a loss, you may need to revise your sales forecast.

Table 4.1 is an example of a monthly sales forecast based on detailed volumes and values over a 12-month period. Alcock's Joinery provides the example, with some assumptions about sales patterns in the carpentry and joinery business.

Table 4.1 Alcock's Joinery Limited: sales forecast for 12 months ending 31 December 1989 (£ thousand)

	Apr.	May	June	July	Aug.	Sept.	Oct.	Nov.	Dec.	Jan.	Feb.	Mar.	Total
Small alcove units	1	1	2	2	2	3	3	1	1	2	4	4	26
Sales value	2.5	2.5	5.0	5.0	5.0	7.5	7.5	2.5	2.5	5.0	10.0	10.0	65.0
Large alcove units	0	0	1	1	1	2	2	0	0	1	2	2	12
Sales value	0	0	5.0	5.0	5.0	10.0	10.0	0	0	5.0	10.0	10.0	60.0
Hours of miscellaneous work	200	200	300	300	400	400	400	100	300	400	500	500	4000
Sales value	2.7	2.7	4.1	4.1	5.5	5.5	5.5	1.5	4.1	5.5	6.9	6.9	55.0
Total sales value	5.2	5.2	14.1	14.1	15.5	23.0	23.0	3.9	6.6	15.5	26.9	26.9	180.0

Alcock's has produced a sales forecast based on the sales pattern over previous years (which we have assumed for the purposes of this example). It can quite clearly be seen that in some months no sales of certain products are envisaged, while in others there appears to be a surge in demand. These seasonal variations are quite realistic and will affect operational decisions as well as cash flow. Not only does the forecast indicate the total sales value expected in 1989, but it also details the volume of products sold, which in turn can be translated into a *capacity forecast* showing the number of hours expected to be worked in each month. This is extremely helpful in deciding how to manage the fluctuations in workload: advance warning means that subcontractors can be organized or new production labour recruited and trained in good time. (We shall not be producing a capacity forecast here, but it should be relatively easy to do so, following the principles established for the sales forecast.)

Forecasting by extrapolating from past trends

This method is appropriate where there is no previous history of sales (such as the launch of a new business or a new activity within an existing one), or where it is possible to build up a forecast based on unit sales. This should be possible in most businesses and will produce the most satisfactory results in terms of accuracy and target setting. But for those businesses where it is not appropriate to break down the sales by product and customer group, sales forecasts will necessarily be based on projecting aggregate figures, rather than the components of the total. In this case, an analysis of sales growth over a period of three to five years is required to produce a sales 'trend', which can then be applied to future sales, adjusted appropriately for changes in internal and external conditions. This is known as 'extrapolation'. Using sales history at Alcock's Joinery as an example:

Year	1983	1984	1985	1986	1987	1988
Sales	£64329	£85674	£99382	£117270	£132898	£154670
Change	–	+33%	+16%	+18%	+13%	+16%

Without knowing anything about the composition of Alcock's sales history, it would be quite reasonable to project sales to 1991 (three years on) at an average annual rate of 16 per cent. This ignores the increase between 1983 and 1984 as being exceptional (a so-called 'outlier'). In other words, if sales were to increase over the next three years as they have done over the past five years, there being no reason for thinking otherwise (such as major economic change), then Alcock's sales forecast *based on a continuation of the base business* for the period to 1991 would be as follows (note how the figures have been rounded up to make the arithmetic easier):

Year	1989	1990	1991
Sales	£180000	£208800	£242200
Change	+16%	+16%	+16%

Using these extrapolations, a monthly forecast for 1989 breaks down the aggregate sales of £180000 into monthly figures by applying a 'factor' to the monthly average (£150000 in 1989) (table 4.2).

The superiority of this method of forecasting monthly sales (over the unit sales method) is that it is based on previous years' sales patterns, which are historically sound. It is also quite simple to produce as long as sales records are available over a number of years. (The well-organized business will be able to enjoy this method.) It is particularly inappropriate, however, when forecasting sales of a new

Table 4.2 Alcock's Joinery Limited: sales forecast for 12 months ending 31 December 1989 (£ thousand)

	Apr.	May	June	July	Aug.	Sept.	Oct.	Nov.	Dec.	Jan.	Feb.	Mar.	Total
Monthly percentage factor	35	35	94	94	103	153	153	26	44	103	179	179	–
Total monthly sales	5.3	5.3	14.1	14.1	15.5	23.0	23.0	3.8	6.6	15.5	26.9	26.9	180.0

Key to sales forecast: monthly percentage factor is based on actual observed factors over recent years, e.g. in April monthly sales are normally 35% of average monthly sales.

business where no history exists, or in cases where the sales history has been very erratic and no regular pattern can be identified. This would apply in the first few years of a new business or where random unpredictable factors affect sales patterns.

It would now be timely to consider the questions 'Is there sufficient customer demand?' and 'Does Alcock's have adequate capacity?' at this point, and to review market research findings and the costs of adding additional capacity to Alcock's workshop. There is also the important question of economic change and whether Alcock's can assume that external influences on demand will remain the same. Since change is inevitable, it may seem unrealistic to forecast using historical patterns only and a more pragmatic approach would almost certainly require an adjustment to sales pattern 'factors' to take into account changes expected in the coming years. Indeed, the company itself might wish to step up sales effort or embark on a totally new direction.

Forecasting with the break-even formula

The planning process should involve consideration of whether the business will be able to support itself financially. Even if profit is not a prime motive, the business will need to generate sufficient income to (at least) cover its costs. At issue here is the question of financial viability: at some point the business moves from loss into profit as the costs of making sales are exceeded by the revenues. The point at which loss turns into profit is called 'break-even' – where profit is zero.

The break-even concept entails consideration of certain cost and revenue issues. The costs of operating the business on an ongoing basis include the following:

1 Costs that the business has to pay anyway, regardless of the level of output or sales activity: these are called *fixed* or *operating* or *overhead costs*. Typically these include rent of premises and other premises costs, wages and salaries, selling and distribution costs and other administrative expenses (these were discussed in detail in chapter 2).

2 Costs that vary in direct proportion with the level of sales: a percentage increase in sales will involve a similar (not always identical) increase in *variable costs*, which typically include materials and stock (in the case of retailers), direct labour time and subcontractors.

The important question here is the actual behaviour of the costs in a particular business. Costs that are fixed in one business may be regarded as variable in another. Thus the test of whether a cost is fixed or variable requires empirical observation.

To achieve financial viability, revenue from sales has to cover both variable costs and fixed costs. Where revenue covers total costs exactly, we have a break-even position, as the following example of a simple profit and loss account based on adjusted 1988 accounts of Alcock's Joinery shows:

Alcock's Joinery Limited
Profit and loss account for break-even sales

	£	%
Sales	133239	(100.0)
Variable costs	77545	(58.2)
Gross profit	55694	(41.8)
Fixed costs	55694	(41.8)
Net profit	0	(0.0)

Alcock's just 'breaks even' where sales revenue (£133239) and total costs (£77545 + £55694 = £133239) are equal, i.e. where net profit is zero. You will notice that fixed costs (£55694) and gross profit margin (41.8 per cent) are the same as the amounts in Alcock's 1988 profit and loss account shown in chapter 2. There is something significant in this observation, as fixed costs and gross profit margin are the two components of the break-even calculation, which is given in the following equations:

$$\text{break-even sales in } \pounds = \frac{\text{fixed costs}}{\text{gross profit margin}}$$

or

$$\text{break-even sales in units} = \frac{\text{fixed costs}}{\text{gross profit}}$$

In an established business, the difficulty is that gross profit margins for the year ahead may not be known, particularly if new products and markets and new production processes and sources of supply are to be introduced, which could change the existing margins by a few percentage points. Therefore calculating the break-even will involve making estimates of the following.

(1) Selling price of a basic or standard sales unit. If selling prices are not known at this point, it is useful to refer to prices being charged by competitors, as it is quite likely that you will not be able to charge prices that are significantly different. We use one of Alcock's basic products as an example:

average price range built-in kitchen unit = £5799 (excl. VAT)

(2) Variable costs (cost of sales) of the basic unit which could be built up from costings or estimated on the basis of comparable products:

materials and consumables	£1350
production labour	£2025
total variable costs	£3375

(3) Gross profit, or 'contribution', of the unit can now be calculated:

selling price	£5799
variable costs	£3375
gross profit	£2424

or 41.8 per cent of sales. This means that every average price range kitchen unit 'contributes' £2424 to the fixed costs of running the

business. If we knew the total level of fixed costs, we could then divide it by the gross profit contribution from each product to give the total number of units that must be sold to cover fixed costs *exactly*.

(4) The fixed costs of running the business for a year must be carefully estimated. This should not prove to be difficult, since the list of fixed costs is finite. The following items are taken from Alcock's profit and loss account, but depending on the type of business there could be many more:

> *selling/distribution costs*
> travel and motor
> advertising
>
> *administration costs*
> rent and rates
> light and heat
> insurance
> repairs and maintenance
> telephone
> printing and stationery
> postage
> general expenses
> audit and accountancy
> salaries
>
> *finance costs*
> bank interest and charges
> depreciation
>
> total fixed costs for the year = £55694

(5) We can now calculate the number of 'contributions' needed to cover the fixed costs for the year (the break-even sales level):

$$\text{break-even sales in units} = \frac{\text{fixed costs}}{\text{gross profit}}$$

$$= \frac{£55694}{£2424}$$

$$= 23 \text{ kitchen units}$$
(or roughly 2 per month)

$$\text{break-even sales in £} = \frac{\text{fixed costs}}{\text{gross profit margin}}$$

$$= \frac{£55694}{41.8\%}$$

$$= £133239$$

(or roughly £11100 per month)

Having calculated the minimum (break-even) sales volume needed, we are in a position to evaluate whether the initial sales plans are realistic. Can the minimum sales level be achieved, or which factors (selling price, variable costs or fixed costs) could be changed to lower the break-even? Bearing in mind that there are no profits at this sales level, you may feel that this is risky and that a lower minimum sales level (a lower break-even) would be more comfortable. To lower the break-even requires one or more of the following actions: reduce total fixed costs, raise unit price or reduce unit variable costs. Reducing fixed costs always seems the obvious option, but in practice it is very difficult to achieve. The largest contributions to fixed costs are salaries and rent, and there are usually no realistic options in these areas. This leaves price and variable costs. The latter also pose problems as there are usually very few improvements in either materials costs or labour costs that can be introduced. To do so would be admitting that you were running production at less than an already high level of efficiency. Therefore the only feasible area for change is raising the selling price which in turn raises gross profit per unit.

Action: raise selling price by 15 per cent on the basis that research shows that customers would not resist a higher price.

average price range built-in kitchen unit = £5799 (excl. VAT)
price raised by 15%   = £6669

materials and consumables = £1350
production labour   = £2025
total variable costs   = £3375 (stays the same)

selling price = £6669
variable costs = £3375
gross profit   = £3294 = 49.4%

$$\text{break-even sales in units} = \frac{\text{fixed costs}}{\text{gross profit}}$$

$$= \frac{£55694}{£3294}$$

$$= \text{17 kitchen units}$$
$$\text{(or roughly 3 every 2 months)}$$

$$\text{break-even sales in } £ = \frac{\text{fixed costs}}{\text{gross profit margin}}$$

$$= \frac{£55694}{49.4\%}$$

$$= £112741$$
$$\text{(or roughly £9400 per month)}$$

A price rise of 15 per cent has resulted in a lower break-even sales level of £9400 per month (down from £11100). If this seems more feasible then it becomes the sales forecast for the year. If not, the process would continue until an acceptable sales level was established, or until the business owner concluded that the business could not be made to work on the basis of the product used in the calculation.

You should now have sales forecasts for the next 12 months on a monthly basis, broken down by product and customer group. In addition, you will also have sales forecasts for years 2 to 5 (or 2 to 3) on an annual basis in aggregate terms (not broken down by product and customer group). Forecasting requires good judgement, which comes from experience. Do not be too optimistic and do not be disappointed if the forecasts do not work out accurately. While achieving 90 per cent accuracy is excellent, try to find out why the forecasts have been inaccurate and apply the lessons learnt to the next round.

Completing the profit and loss accounts

Forecasts of variable costs and overheads should be based on financial ratios and relationships established from historical accounts (as we saw in the case of Alcock's and SCS in chapter 3), adjusted appropriately for anticipated changes in the planning period. A detailed monthly budget for the next 12 months should then be constructed from the forecasts, based on sales and related costs of sales in the year.

The starting point is to list the last five years' profit and loss accounts in parallel columns, expressing *every cost item* as a percentage of sales (exactly as we did in chapter 3), although only where the cost item is significant, i.e. where the cost is less than 1 per cent of sales, it is too insignificant to express as a percentage of sales.

This should establish trends in expenditure patterns, particularly with regard to the major cost areas, i.e. cost of sales, selling and distribution expenses, administration expenses, salaries, finance expenses and depreciation. With the sales revenues for each year of the planning period already calculated, the gross profit and net profit percentages for each year established in the corporate plan as part of the process of setting business objectives and the expenditure trends established for the past five years, we can now complete the forecast profit and loss accounts. The forecasting sequence is as follows.

1 Lay out the profit and loss accounts for the next three years in parallel columns, following the normal format illustrated in chapter 2 it might be necessary to lay out each year in *one* column, rather than in two, simply because of space considerations).
2 Enter the sales forecasts in each year.
3 Enter gross profit and net profit before tax in each year, using the percentage margins decided on earlier.
4 Using the main expenditure percentages established from previous years (cost of sales, selling and distribution expenses, administration expenses, finance expenses), adjusted for proposed changes in the planning period, calculate the main expenditure categories for each of the three years. It is likely that further adjustments will be needed at this point in order to make them 'fit' the profit and loss account and a compromise might have to be reached between expenditure and objectives. It is usual at this point to re-examine corporate objectives in the light of the preliminary forecasts.
5 Using the trend percentages established from previous years and adjusting them for proposed changes, complete the profit and loss accounts by calculating the expenditure details within each main

expenditure category. Again some further adjustments might be required.

Alcock's profit and loss accounts and balance sheets for the last two years, with expenditure percentages, are shown in tables 4.3 and 4.4 (these are exactly the same as the accounts shown in chapter 2).

We observe a fairly steady relationship between the main expenditure items and sales income. The relationships and ratios in the main expenditure categories were discussed in chapter 3 and we can now use these relationships to assist with Alcock's projected accounts (table 4.5). These forecasts were developed using the relationships (trends) established in the historical accounts. An explanation of these forecasts is as follows.

1 *Sales* are projected at an increase of 16 per cent per annum.
2 *Gross profit margin* is projected to rise slightly from 41.8 per cent to 43 per cent, 44 per cent, 45 per cent, as part of a deliberate policy to raise prices and cut out unprofitable lines.
3 *Net profit margin* is projected at 6.2 per cent, 7.1 per cent and 8.1 per cent of sales following the objectives set in the corporate plan.
4 *Materials* showed a declining trend over previous years. This trend is continued.
5 *Stock* is projected at a steady 40 days of purchases, which is close to the 'stock days' trend established in chapter 3. Note that closing stock becomes opening stock in the following year.
6 *Direct labour* forecasts are based on salary increases of 5 per cent each year plus one additional joiner at £7000 each year (£8000 in 1991).
7 *Subcontractors* are forecast to decline slowly as part of company policy on using internal resources.
8 *Selling and distribution expenses* are projected at 7 per cent of sales, following the historical trend. Within these, travel (4.5 per cent) and advertising (2.5 per cent) are assumed to remain constant.
9 *Administration expenses* are projected at 26 per cent of sales. Rent is due to be raised to £12900 in 1989 and is projected to grow at 10 per cent per annum thereafter and all other expenses by nominal amounts (it is not worth expressing these small amounts as percentages of sales), except salaries, which are projected to

Table 4.3 Alcock's Joinery Limited: profit and loss account for the year ending 31 March 1988

	1988 £	%	1987 £	%
Sales	154670	100	132898	100
Cost of sales				
Materials	35290	22.8	31045	23.3
+ Opening stock and WIP	2130		1890	
	37420		32935	
− Closing stock and WIP	3790		2130	
	33630		30805	
Direct labour	46750	30.2	37400	28.1
Subcontractors	9500		6350	
	89880		74555	
Gross profit	64790	41.8	58343	43.9
Selling expenses				
Travel and motor	6653	4.3	6579	5.0
Advertising	4218	2.7	3709	2.8
	10871	7.0	10288	7.8
Administration expenses				
Rent and rates	10500	6.8	10500	7.9
Light and heat	808	0.5	768	0.6
Insurance	560	0.4	450	0.3
Repairs and maintenance	962	0.6	1008	0.8
Telephone	895	0.6	768	0.6
Printing and stationery	1790	1.2	1670	1.3
Postage	679	0.4	387	0.3
General expenses	846	0.5	657	0.5
Audit and accountancy	795	0.5	750	0.6
Salaries and NIC	20560	13.3	19760	14.9
	38395	24.8	36718	27.6
Finance expenses				
Bank interest	1410	0.9	1424	1.1
Bank charges	378	0.2	356	0.2
	1788	1.1	1780	1.3
Depreciation	4640	3.0	4470	3.4
	55694		53256	
Net profit	9096	5.8	5087	3.8
Taxation	2445	1.6	1831	1.4
Transferred to reserves	6651		3256	

Table 4.4 Alcock's Joinery Limited: balance sheet at 31 March

	1988 £	Ratio	1987 £	Ratio
FIXED ASSETS				
Equipment and machinery	39760		33685	
Motor vehicle	8900		8900	
	48660		42585	
Less: depreciation	34091		29451	
	14569	£10.61	13134	£10.11
CURRENT ASSETS				
Stock and WIP	3790	39 d	2130	25 d
Debtors	16863	40 d	13203	36 d
Cash	3481		600	
	24134		15933	
Less: CURRENT LIABILITIES				
Trade creditors	6285	65 d	5188	61 d
Sundry creditors	6295	4.1%	4385	3.3%
Taxation	2445		1831	
Overdraft	2503		576	
	17528		11980	
NET CURRENT ASSETS	6606	1.24x	3953	1.09x
NET ASSETS	21175		17087	
FINANCED BY				
Share capital	2000		2000	
Profit and loss account	11261		4610	
	13261		6610	
Bank loan	7914		10477	
Capital employed	21175		17087	

	Equipment	Vehicle	Total
Value of assets at cost			
At 31 March 1987	33685	8900	42585
Acquired during year	6075	0	6075
At 31 March 1988	39760	8900	48660
Depreciation	@ 25%	@ 20%	
To 31 March 1987	23755	5696	29451
During year	4000	640	4640
To 31 March 1988	27755	6336	34091

Table 4.5 Alcock's Joinery Limited: projected profit and loss accounts for the years ending 31 March

	1989 £	%	1990 £	%	1991 £	%
Sales	180000	100	208800	100	242200	100
Cost of sales						
Materials	38700	21.5	43800	21.0	49600	20.5
Opening stock and WIP	3790		4240		4920	
Closing stock and WIP	4240		4920		5300	
Direct labour	56100		65900		77200	
Subcontractors	8250		7880		6780	
	102600	57	116900	56	133200	55
Gross profit	77400	43	91900	44	109000	45
Selling expenses						
Travel and motor	8100	4.5	9400	4.5	10900	4.5
Advertising	4500	2.5	5200	2.5	6100	2.5
	12600	7	14600	7	17000	7
Administration expenses						
Rent and rates	12900		14200		15600	
Light and heat	1200		1400		1600	
Insurance	600		700		800	
Repairs/maintenance	1400		1500		1600	
Telephone	1000		1200		1400	
Printing/stationery	1900		2100		2300	
Postage	800		1000		1200	
General expenses	900		1000		1100	
Audit/accountancy	900		1100		1300	
Salaries and NIC	25200		30100		36100	
	46800	26	54300	26	63000	26
Finance expenses						
Bank interest	1400		1600		1800	
Bank charges	400		500		600	
	1800	1	2100	1	2400	1
Depreciation	5000		6000		7000	
Expenditure	66200		77000		89400	
Net profit	11200	6.2	14900	7.1	19600	8.1
Taxation	2800		3700		4900	
Transfer to reserves	8400		11200		14700	

grow at 5 per cent per annum plus a small amount for additional office overheads each year. (The exact amount is variable as the salaries have been used as a balancing item in the projections.)

10 *Finance expenses* are projected at 1 per cent of sales, which is roughly in line with the trend. Bank interest and charges are based on no additional borrowing and therefore are increased by a small amount each year.

11 *Depreciation* is projected to increase by a small amount each year.

12 *Corporation tax* is assumed to be payable at 25 per cent of net profit each year. (The exact amount can only be calculated once allowable and disallowable expenses and capital allowances have been settled.)

Producing budgeted monthly profit and loss accounts

Having produced and explained the annual profit and loss account forecasts, we are now in a position to produce monthly profit and loss accounts – or budgets – for 1989. Budgets flow naturally from annual forecasts, which is why we dealt with the latter first. They are used principally as a guide to the desired levels of sales income and expenditure in the various functional areas of the business – in each of the profit and loss account sales and expenditure categories – and are a very necessary method of monitoring how actual income and expenditure deviate from planned levels. Deviations, or variances, are one way of measuring whether the business is likely to make planned profits and if not, whether income or expenditure is at fault, and if the latter, which expenditure items are to blame.

Like most forecasting, breaking down the annual income and expenditure amounts is a matter of experience, although some help for first timers can be provided by having available records of monthly income and expenditure levels from previous years. We have already produced monthly income forecasts, using either the forecast of unit sales to sales value method, or the 'factor' application method, described earlier. We can enter these monthly sales figures into our budgeted profit and loss account and forecast expenditure against each sales volume on a monthly basis.

Alcock's monthly budget for 1989 (table 4.6) is based firmly on

Table 4.6 Alcock's Joinery Limited: budgeted profit and loss account: April 1988–March 1989 (£ thousand)

	Apr	May	Jun	Jul	Aug	Sep	Oct	Nov	Dec	Jan	Feb	Mar	Total
Sales income	5.3	5.3	14.1	14.1	15.5	23.0	23.0	3.8	6.6	15.5	26.9	26.9	180.0
Materials	1.2	1.2	3.0	3.0	3.3	4.9	4.9	0.9	1.4	3.3	5.8	5.8	38.7
+Opening stock	3.8	3.8	3.9	3.9	4.0	4.0	4.1	4.1	4.2	4.2	4.2	4.2	3.8
−Closing stock	3.8	3.9	3.9	4.0	4.0	4.1	4.1	4.2	4.2	4.2	4.2	4.2	4.2
Direct labour	4.6	4.6	4.6	4.7	4.7	4.7	4.7	4.7	4.7	4.7	4.7	4.7	56.1
Subcontractors	0.6	0.6	0.7	0.7	0.7	0.7	0.7	0.7	0.7	0.7	0.7	0.7	8.2
	6.4	6.3	8.3	8.3	8.7	10.2	10.3	6.2	6.8	8.7	11.2	11.2	102.6
Gross profit	(1.1)	(1.0)	5.8	5.8	6.8	12.8	12.7	(2.4)	(0.2)	6.8	15.7	15.7	77.4
Travel	0.6	0.6	0.6	0.7	0.7	0.7	0.7	0.7	0.7	0.7	0.7	0.7	8.1
Advertising	0.3	0.3	0.3	0.4	0.4	0.4	0.4	0.4	0.4	0.4	0.4	0.4	4.5
Rent and rates	1.0	1.0	1.0	1.1	1.1	1.1	1.1	1.1	1.1	1.1	1.1	1.1	12.9
Electricity	0.1	0.1	0.1	0.1	0.1	0.1	0.1	0.1	0.1	0.1	0.1	0.1	1.2
Insurance	0.0	0.1	0.0	0.1	0.0	0.1	0.0	0.1	0.0	0.1	0.0	0.1	0.6
Repairs	0.1	0.1	0.1	0.1	0.1	0.2	0.1	0.1	0.1	0.1	0.1	0.2	1.4
Telephone	0.0	0.1	0.1	0.1	0.1	0.1	0.0	0.1	0.1	0.1	0.1	0.1	1.0
Printing	0.1	0.1	0.2	0.1	0.2	0.2	0.1	0.2	0.2	0.1	0.2	0.2	1.9
Post and stationery	0.0	0.1	0.0	0.1	0.0	0.1	0.0	0.1	0.1	0.1	0.1	0.1	0.8
General expenses	0.1	0.1	0.1	0.0	0.1	0.1	0.1	0.0	0.1	0.1	0.1	0.0	0.9
Accountancy and audit	0.1	0.1	0.1	0.0	0.1	0.1	0.1	0.0	0.1	0.1	0.1	0.0	0.9
Salaries and NIC	2.1	2.1	2.1	2.1	2.1	2.1	2.1	2.1	2.1	2.1	2.1	2.1	25.2
Interest	0.1	0.1	0.1	0.1	0.1	0.2	0.1	0.1	0.1	0.1	0.1	0.2	1.4
Bank charges	0.0	0.0	0.1	0.0	0.0	0.1	0.0	0.0	0.1	0.0	0.0	0.1	0.4
Depreciation	0.4	0.4	0.4	0.4	0.4	0.4	0.4	0.4	0.4	0.4	0.5	0.5	5.0
Total expenditure	5.0	5.3	5.4	5.5	5.6	6.0	5.3	5.5	5.7	5.6	5.7	5.9	66.2
Net profit/loss	(6.1)	(6.3)	0.5	0.4	1.3	6.8	7.4	(7.9)	(5.9)	1.2	10.0	9.8	11.2
Accumulated profit/loss	(6.1)	(12.4)	(11.9)	(11.5)	(10.2)	(3.4)	4.0	(3.9)	(9.8)	(8.6)	1.4	11.2	

the extrapolated forecasts for the three year planning period. The total column on the right-hand side agrees with the forecast profit and loss account shown earlier. Individual monthly budgets are calculated broadly as follows: variable costs (cost of sales) including materials, labour and subcontractors are by definition directly proportional to sales and are therefore calculated in the same factor proportions as were used to produce the monthly sales forecast, whereas fixed costs, or expenditure overheads, are simply divided into 12 equal, or roughly equal, monthly amounts. More specifically, the budgeted monthly profit and loss account is calculated in the following way:

1 *Sales* are taken from the monthly sales forecast calculated earlier.
2 *Materials* are apportioned in the same way as monthly sales. Stock hardly changes at all over the year and the gradual increase is shown (arbitrarily) each quarter. The use of arbitrary forecasting methods can be condoned in cases where either there is

insufficient information on which to base an extrapolation or the amounts are insignificant. The latter is the case in our example: stock grows over the year by some £400, which is small in relation to other changes in the business.

3 *Direct labour* is not apportioned in relation to sales, as the workforce has to be paid regardless of output. Total annual salaries are divided into 12 roughly equal monthly amounts, allowing for rounding of the amounts to the nearest thousand pounds.

4 *Subcontractors* amount to only a small sum and are simply divided into 12 monthly amounts.

5 *Gross profit* varies considerably over the year. In the early months the company is making a gross *loss*, as sales are low and salaries are more or less fixed in relation to output.

6 *Selling, administration and finance* expenses are calculated in the same way. They are spread evenly over the 12 months on the assumption that they are totally (or predominantly) fixed in relation to sales. Certain expenses are semi-fixed, in the sense that part varies directly with sales and part is fixed. In these cases, it is safer and simpler to regard them as fixed.

7 *Net profit or loss* is calculated on a monthly as well as an accumulative (running total) basis and shows how volatile profitability can be. In four of the months the company makes a loss and in nine there is an accumulated loss.

At this point the obvious course of action is to review the annual and monthly profit and loss forecasts in the light of the losses incurred over several months. There is nothing wrong with such a review, and the outcomes shown in Alcock's forecasts are typical of a business of this type and are entirely realistic. Furthermore, it is appropriate at this stage to reconsider the forecasts and the assumptions on which they are built, having identified the unevenness of profit accumulation. By retracing our steps to the sales forecasts we can see why Alcock's has fluctuating profit. Everything stems from the sales forecast which underlines the vital importance attached to accurate and realistic sales forecasting. The challenge now is to produce a sales forecast that generates profit on a regular basis, or at least reduces losses in certain months of the year. This may not be easy, and in the final analysis the problem can be traced back to the company's markets and its marketing strategy. At this point an entire review of strategy may be warranted and the corporate plan redrafted.

Cash flow forecasting

Cash flow forecasting is undoubtedly the most widely discussed financial document in the area of small business management. The purpose of a cash flow forecast is to identify *how much* cash the business will need over the coming 12 months and *when* additional facilities will be needed. This is achieved by forecasting cash banked each month and subtracting from these amounts cash paid out by the business. The process is as follows:

cash paid into the bank in the course of a month (cash received from sales + loans + grants)

less

cash paid out to creditors in the course of the same month (cash paid to suppliers, landlords, employees, petty cash expenses, VAT, taxation, equipment suppliers, banks)

equals

cash flow, either into or out of the bank account during the month, depending on whichever is larger (cash paid in or paid out).

The concept of cash flow is therefore a simple one and can easily be represented diagrammatically:

BANK BALANCE (CURRENT & DEPOSIT ACCOUNTS)

+ CASH RECEIVED AND BANKED (FROM ANY SOURCE)

− CASH PAID OUT (TO ANY RECIPIENT)

= (NEW) BANK BALANCE

This flow of cash into and out of the bank account takes place hourly, daily, weekly and monthly, but it is conventional to forecast cash flow on a monthly basis (although certain businesses may need to forecast cash requirements more frequently). The above diagram illustrates an important feature of the cash flow forecast: we are trying to forecast the business's *bank balance*. By keeping the bank balance under control the business will always be in a position to pay its bills and therefore remain solvent. We return to the issue of financial control in chapter 5.

Most well-managed businesses these days produce a cash flow forecast. Therefore the issue is not in dispute. The difficulty lies in producing a meaningful forecast – in other words, where there is an acceptable balance between accuracy and effort. Since forecasts are almost always wrong in their outcomes, the issue is not 'how to produce an accurate forecast' but rather 'how to produce a realistic forecast that reliably identifies financial requirements'. The end product is not the accuracy of the forecasts but rather the adequacy of finance for business development. The cash flow forecast does not identify what types of finance are most suitable; we deal with financial sources in chapter 6.

There is always confusion between *cash flow* and *profit*. The essence of profit and loss accounts, which show income and expenditure over a period, is that they are produced on an *invoiced* basis. In other words, income is recorded in the period in which it is invoiced (the realization concept) and expenditure is related to that income also on an invoiced basis, but adjusted for accruals and prepayments (the accrual concept). These concepts determine that income and expenditure be included in the accounts *whether or not we have received or paid out cash* for them.

Therein lies the fundamental difference between profit and cash. Cash flow treats income and expenditure *not* on an invoiced basis, but solely on a *cash paid* basis. Because of this difference, cash flow is a wider concept than profit and loss. There are many instances where cash is paid which do not give rise to an entry in the profit and loss account. One such example is VAT. We know that we receive VAT from our customers and pay it to our suppliers, paying the balance to the Department of Customs and Excise, yet it does not appear in the profit and loss account (it does not belong to the business, but rather to the government). It is a cash item only.

In order to understand the principles of cash flow forecasting and the difference between cash and profit, we draw on Alcock's as an example. Cash flow forecasts are based on the cash transactions related to day-to-day business activity, whether this be sales invoiced to customers, purchases made from suppliers or other typical transactions. Most of these transactions have already been detailed in the forecast profit and loss accounts for the period 1989–1991. We may need to review these transactions and possibly add to them, but they constitute a useful starting point for the cash flow forecasting activity.

Before starting the exercise, a few preparatory steps are necessary:

1 Prepare budgeted monthly profit and loss accounts (we did this earlier).
2 Have available records of money owed to suppliers and other creditors (such as VAT, PAYE and tax) at the start of the year (from last year's accounts) and money owed by customers (debtors from the balance sheet).
3 Decide on assumptions about *credit payment periods* both from customers and to suppliers. You will need to translate invoiced amounts from the profit and loss account into payments in the cash flow.
4 Review purchases of plant, equipment and vehicles for inclusion in the cash flow forecast and methods of financing them.

We are now ready to produce a cash flow forecast (table 4.7). The format for the forecast below is based on the projected profit and loss account with several significant changes, mainly the inclusion of a number of cash items not previously covered explicitly in the profit and loss account. There is no one way to produce a cash flow, however, and the following is merely a recommended format. Adapt the forecast to suit your individual needs.

Keeping in view the purpose of the exercise (to determine short-term financing needs), observe how cash at the bank is negative for most of the year, moving into surplus only in the final month, leaving a cash balance of £7200 in the bank account. This amount is shown in the forecast balance sheet for the year (to be demonstrated shortly). These forecasts result in the business 'going into the red' in the period April to February. Note that the balance sheet shows *only the year end* cash or overdraft amounts and not cash requirements during the year, which is quite misleading, as our example shows. This is the main reason a monthly (rather than a quarterly or bi-monthly) cash flow forecast is needed.

An explanation of the forecasting procedures is as follows:

Table 4.7 Alcock's Joinery Limited: cash flow forecast April 1988–March 1989 (£ thousand)

	Apr	May	Jun	Jul	Aug	Sep	Oct	Nov	Dec	Jan	Feb	Mar	Total
CASH IN													
Deposits	1.7	1.7	4.6	4.6	5.1	7.6	7.6	1.2	2.2	5.1	8.9	8.9	59.2
Balance	16.9	3.6	3.6	9.5	9.5	10.4	15.4	15.4	2.6	4.4	10.4	18.0	119.7
Output VAT	0.8	0.8	2.1	2.1	2.3	3.5	3.5	0.6	1.0	2.3	4.0	4.0	27.0
Brought forward	1.0												1.0
Total cash in	20.4	6.1	10.3	16.2	16.9	21.5	26.5	17.2	5.8	11.8	23.3	30.9	206.9
CASH OUT													
Materials	5.2	1.2	1.2	3.0	3.0	3.3	4.9	4.9	0.9	1.4	3.3	5.8	38.1
Direct labour	4.6	4.6	4.6	4.7	4.7	4.7	4.7	4.7	4.7	4.7	4.7	4.7	56.1
Subcontractors	0.8	0.6	0.6	0.7	0.7	0.7	0.7	0.7	0.7	0.7	0.7	0.7	8.3
Travel	0.6	0.6	0.6	0.7	0.7	0.7	0.7	0.7	0.7	0.7	0.7	0.7	8.1
Advertising	0.3	0.3	0.3	0.3	0.4	0.4	0.4	0.4	0.4	0.4	0.4	0.4	4.4
Rent and rates	1.0	1.0	1.0	1.1	1.1	1.1	1.1	1.1	1.1	1.1	1.1	1.1	12.9
Electricity	0.0	0.3	0.0	0.0	0.3	0.0	0.0	0.3	0.0	0.0	0.3	0.0	1.2
Insurance	0.0	0.0	0.0	0.6	0.0	0.0	0.0	0.0	0.0	0.0	0.0	0.0	0.6
Repairs	0.1	0.1	0.1	0.1	0.1	0.2	0.1	0.1	0.1	0.1	0.1	0.2	1.4
Telephone	0.0	0.0	0.2	0.0	0.0	0.2	0.0	0.0	0.3	0.0	0.0	0.3	1.0
Printing	0.1	0.1	0.2	0.1	0.2	0.2	0.1	0.2	0.2	0.1	0.2	0.2	1.9
Post and stationery	0.0	0.1	0.0	0.1	0.0	0.1	0.0	0.1	0.1	0.1	0.1	0.1	0.8
General expenses	0.1	0.1	0.1	0.0	0.1	0.1	0.1	0.0	0.1	0.1	0.1	0.0	0.9
Accountancy and audit	0.0	0.0	0.0	0.0	0.0	0.0	0.9	0.0	0.0	0.0	0.0	0.0	0.9
Salaries and NIC	2.1	2.1	2.1	2.1	2.1	2.1	2.1	2.1	2.1	2.1	2.1	2.1	25.2
Interest	0.0	0.0	0.3	0.0	0.0	0.4	0.0	0.0	0.3	0.0	0.0	0.4	1.4
Bank charges	0.0	0.0	0.1	0.0	0.0	0.1	0.0	0.0	0.1	0.0	0.0	0.1	0.4
Loan repayments	0.0	0.0	0.4	0.0	0.0	0.5	0.0	0.0	0.4	0.0	0.0	0.5	1.8
Equipment	0.0	0.0	3.0	0.0	0.0	0.0	0.0	0.0	0.0	3.0	0.0	0.0	6.0
Taxation	5.4	0.0	0.0	0.0	0.0	0.0	0.0	0.0	0.0	0.0	0.0	0.0	5.4
Input VAT	1.1	0.4	0.9	0.7	0.7	0.8	1.2	1.0	0.5	0.9	0.8	1.2	10.2
VAT to C&E	3.3	0.0	0.0	1.3	0.0	0.0	5.7	0.0	0.0	2.4	0.0	0.0	12.7
Total cash out	24.7	11.5	15.7	15.5	14.1	15.6	22.7	16.3	12.7	17.8	14.6	18.5	199.7
Cash flow	(4.3)	(5.4)	(5.4)	0.7	2.8	5.9	3.8	0.9	(6.9)	(6.0)	8.7	12.4	7.2
Bank balance	(4.3)	(9.7)	(15.1)	(14.4)	(11.6)	(5.7)	(1.9)	(1.0)	(7.9)	(13.9)	(5.2)	7.2	

(1) *Cash from sales* is divided into cash received from a one-third deposit required of customers when they place the order and the balance of two-thirds payable on completion of the work, which is assumed to be in the month following the order. No credit is given to the mainly domestic customers. Therefore the method is to take sales income from the monthly sales forecast, calculate one-third as the deposit paid in the same month as the sale is made and another two-thirds as the balance paid in the following month. These amounts are entered throughout the year, *bringing forward from March 1988* the two-thirds balance payable on orders taken in December (debtors of £16900 found in the 1988 balance sheet) and *carrying forward as creditors the balances owing in April 1990 (£18000)*. These creditors are to be found in the forecast balance sheets.

(2) *VAT* at 15 per cent is received from each sale and is paid out on those expenditure categories which fall within the scope of VAT; it is itemized separately in the cash flow forecast. It is possible to produce a cash flow where all the payments are shown gross as they actually happen. It is not recommended, however, because it has the following results:

(a) it makes the VAT arithmetic more complicated;
(b) it makes the production of profit and loss accounts and balance sheets significantly more difficult.

There are a number of reasons for treating VAT separately. Although VAT disappears from the business's overall trading accounts (it is collected for and paid to the government), it can have a significant effect on cash needs, particularly if substantial amounts are spent on equipment and stock at certain times of the year and extended credit is granted to customers.

VAT complicates the arithmetic, since the amounts are generally not round numbers and it is advisable to adjust the VAT figures so that they too end in zeros. Although VAT is shown separately in the example, the actual cheques received and issued will of course include VAT. Separating their components out in the cash flow makes the calculations easier, and does not affect the result because it is the overall effect of the month's transactions which is being calculated.

Working out VAT can be confusing because prices for business (trade prices) are usually quoted without VAT, whereas consumer (retail) prices are quoted including VAT. The fraction used for calculating VAT on gross amounts is:

$$\frac{15}{115} = \frac{3}{23}$$

or multiply the gross amount by 0.1304.

The treatment of VAT in our example has been partly simplified in accordance with new VAT rules (October 1988) allowing calculations on a cash basis (calculations are still permissible on an invoiced basis). VAT on sales has been calculated on an invoiced basis whereas VAT on expenditure has been calculated on the following items on a cash basis (since not all expenditure incurs

VAT): materials, subcontractors, travel, advertising, repairs, telephone, printing, accountancy and equipment.

For a given VAT period (three months), the total of VAT on payments invoiced is calculated, as is the total of VAT on payments made. These are shown separately each month and are known respectively as *output VAT* and *input VAT*. The difference is payable to (or receivable from) the Department of Customs and Excise one month after the end of the VAT period and these amounts too are shown in the forecast in the line 'C&E'. VAT due to Customs and Excise in April 1990 (output VAT minus input VAT over the last three months of 1989) amounts to £7400 and will be shown as a sundry creditor in the forecast balance sheet.

(3) *Cash brought forward* from March 1988 is added to cash received from various sources (only sales in our example) to give a total for cash banked each month.

(4) *Materials* payments are forecast on the basis of being due 30 days later (the month following purchase). Creditors of £5200 from March 1988 are brought forward (£6300 less subcontractors of £800 and advertising of £300 owing from 1988) for payment in April and creditors due for payment in April 1990 are carried forward (£5800).

(5) *Direct labour* is paid at the end of each month and therefore the amounts can be transferred from the profit and loss account.

(6) *Subcontractors* payments are based on being due 30 days from date of invoice. Amounts owed from March 1988 (£800) are brought forward for payment in April and amounts owed in April 1990 (£700) are taken into the forecast balance sheet.

(7) *Advertising* expenditure is paid for 30 days after invoice date. Amounts owed from March 1988 (£300) are brought forward for payment in April and amounts owed at the end of March 1989 (£400) are carried into the balance sheet.

(8) The remaining *overheads* are assumed to be paid within the year: there are no further adjustments for creditors, which is not quite realistic since certain bills will be payable in the next financial year (such as electricity). These will be small amounts only and will not materially affect the cash outcomes. *Electricity* is paid quarterly, *insurance* in April (when the bill will probably arrive), *repairs* are

cash items, *telephone* quarterly, *printing* the same month, *post* and *general expenses* are cash items, *accountancy and audit* fees are paid in July, *salaries* are paid monthly, *loan interest, bank charges* and *loan repayments* are paid quarterly, *equipment* is paid for when it is acquired, and *taxation* is due on 1 April and includes corporation and income taxes due (£5400).

There are a number of general principles of cash flow forecasting which, if observed, will simplify the task and increase accuracy:

(1) *Accuracy and realism* are important principles to observe when calculating large amounts (which will materially affect the outcomes) but small sums should not unduly occupy the forecaster's time. Equally, since forecasts are never 100 per cent correct, use as many zeros as possible, rounding the forecasts to the nearest 100 or 1000.

(2) *Checking for accuracy* should be undertaken frequently. Unless using a spreadsheet to generate the cash flows (which is to be encouraged, given the time that it will save in the future), forecasts should be checked for accuracy at every opportunity. Since the forecast is based on horizontal rows and vertical columns, totalling in both directions is an easy way to check the arithmetical accuracy of rows and columns. Checking should be done when totalling *cash in, cash out* and *bank balance* since at these points horizontal and vertical calculations produce a common answer. Errors in the cash flow forecast will prevent the balancing of projected balance sheets.

(3) *Caution rather than optimism* should be the guiding principle when forecasting cash flow. While the general rule is that amounts in the cash flows should be entered in the months in which they are actually to be paid out or banked, if there is any doubt about when amounts fall due, then it is preferable to err on the side of caution. For example, if customers are wont to ignore the agreed terms (say 30 days) because they pay their bills at a certain time in the month, the receipts from sales should be entered on the assumption that they will be paid in 60 days, not 30. On the expenditure side the reverse should always apply: if there is any doubt about a payment to a supplier, then assume that it should be paid as soon as possible.

Most cash flow forecasting is over-optimistic. This could result in an under-assessment of short-term financing needs, which in turn could lead to a shortage of funds. While sales receipts suffer from the problem of late payment, payments suffer in three areas: costs tend to be *higher* than expected, there tend to be *more cost categories* than was originally assumed and costs have a habit of happening *sooner* than anticipated. In combination, these factors can produce difficulties even for the well-managed business and the lesson is to forecast on a mildly pessimistic basis.

(4) *Changes and improvements* will always be needed before the forecast can be accepted. Cash flow forecasts rarely work out perfectly the first time. Like the rest of the forecasting process, changes are often required in order to strike a balance between the ability of the business owner to organize the people, production, marketing and finance, and the financial requirements to support this organization. In our example, Alcock's would be overdrawn to £12100 in the early part of 1989. If the bank will not accept this level of debt, the cash flows will have to be re-calculated on a different set of assumptions, one of which will almost certainly be a different sales forecast. Thus the entire forecasting process will have to be subjected to a rigorous re-examination. Forecasting is an iterative experiential process and should not be treated too scientifically.

Alcock's Joinery is set to enjoy a modestly profitable year with ample funds in the bank by the end of it, according to our forecasts. Net profit after tax will be £8400 and cash at the bank £13600. This demonstrates clearly that *cash and profit are not the same thing.* This difference is accounted for as follows:

Cash flow forecast	*Profit and loss account*
Payments by customers	Invoices to customers
Payments to suppliers	Bills from suppliers
VAT	No VAT
Equipment	Depreciation
Taxation paid	Taxation due (no expense)
Loans received	No loans received
Loan repayments	No loan repayments
No stock and work in progress	Stock and WIP

Most of these issues have been covered in the text. It is important to note that profit and cash are not the same, since it is quite possible to get into financial difficulties (run out of cash) while still making a profit. The reasons for such a state of affairs can be seen in the list.

Imagine the following scenario: a company has run up an overdraft to the limit of its facility. Creditors are pressing for payment at the same time and just at this moment taxation and VAT payments are due (and incur penalties for late payment). Although sales are being invoiced rapidly, customers take their full credit period and more, paying sometimes 60 days after date of invoice. There is no time to follow up late payers. Therefore no cash comes in. Staff need paying and the landlord is pressing for the rent.

These are familiar circumstances: the business makes a profit but cannot generate enough cash to meet short-term debts. The result is legal action by creditors and eventually a winding-up order against the company, despite a profitable trading history. The answer lies in the appropriate actions to generate simultaneously profit and sufficient cash to meet short-term needs. These actions are a matter of financial control, which we deal with in the next chapter. But they have their origins in the distinction between cash and profit and a thorough understanding of these differences is vital for effective financial management.

Forecasting balance sheets

The balance sheet is probably the easiest financial statement to forecast, but requires a thorough understanding of the financial ratios discussed in chapter 3. They can be applied more or less mechanically to a given set of figures: these figures appear already in the profit and loss accounts and cash flow forecast, which are an indispensable base for the forecasting process. This process starts with sales forecasts and ends with the balance sheets:

ANNUAL SALES FORECASTS FOR PLANNING PERIOD
↓
MONTHLY SALES FORECASTS FOR FIRST YEAR
↓
PROFIT AND LOSS ACCOUNT FORECASTS FOR
PLANNING PERIOD
↓
BUDGET MONTHLY PROFIT AND LOSS ACCOUNT FOR
FIRST YEAR
↓
MONTHLY CASH FLOW FORECAST FOR FIRST YEAR
↓
BALANCE SHEET FORECASTS FOR PLANNING PERIOD

The purpose of forecasting balance sheets for the planning period is to determine the longer-term financing needs of the business in order to be able to assess the relative contributions required of internally generated finance (profit, improved cash controls) and finance from external sources. Since the discipline of tighter financial control is likely to take some time to embed itself in the company (particularly if there is no culture of tight control), it is vital to take a longer-term view of financial needs.

Based on the corporate plan for the period 1989 to 1991, two years' historical balance sheets, forecasts of profit for the next three years and a cash flow forecast for the next 12 months, Alcock's forecast balance sheets for the planning period are shown in table 4.8.

The projected balance sheets are built up on the fundamental premise that balance sheets must balance. In other words, having established one side of the equation, the other side must equal it. This makes forecasting balance sheets relatively easy, as long as we have an adequate knowledge of the key financial ratios, i.e. sales income to fixed assets, stock days, debtor days and creditor days.

Alcock's balance sheets have been projected on the basis of the following assumptions, which are in turn based on historical evidence (previous years' balance sheets) and various agreed policies on financial control procedures:

(1) *Fixed assets* net of depreciation: in 1989 we established the need for £6000 of new equipment (see the cash flow forecast) which would be spent in two tranches of £3000. The depreciation charge of £5000 is calculated as follows (and has already appeared in the profit and loss forecasts):

Fixed assets at cost	Equipment	Vehicle	Total
At 31 March 1988	39760	8900	48660
Acquired during year	6000	0	6000
At 31 March 1989	45760	8900	54660

Depreciation	@ 25%	@ 20%	Total
To 31 March 1988	27755	6336	34091
During year	4500	500	5000
To 31 March 1989	32255	6836	39091

Table 4.8 Alcock's Joinery Limited: projected balance sheets at 31 March

	1989 £		1990 £		1991 £	
FIXED ASSETS						
Net book value	15600	£11.54	17400	£12.00	19400	£12.50
CURRENT ASSETS						
Stock and WIP	4200	40 d	4800	40 d	5400	40 d
Debtors	18000	36 d	20600	36 d	23900	36 d
Cash	7200		14500		25400	
	29400		39900		54700	
Less:						
CURRENT LIABILITIES						
Trade creditors	6900	65 d	7800	65 d	8800	65 d
Sundry creditors	9300	5%	10400	5%	12100	5%
Taxation	2800		3700		4900	
Overdraft	0		0		0	
	19000		21900		25800	
NET CURRENT ASSETS	10400		18000		28900	
NET ASSETS	26000		35400		48300	
FINANCED BY						
Share capital	2000		2000		2000	
Profit and loss account	19700		30900		45600	
	21700		32900		47600	
Bank loan	4300		2500		700	
Capital employed	26000		35400		48300	

The calculation of depreciation was discussed in chapter 2 and we use the same method here. (For the opening fixed asset position, refer to Alcock's balance sheets in chapter 2.) The annual depreciation of £5000 is calculated as follows:

equipment at cost at 31 March 1989	£45760
less accumulated depreciation to 31 March 1988	£27755
net book value before 1989 depreciation	£18005
1989 depreciation @ 25%	£4501

vehicle at cost at 31 March 1989	£8900
less accumulated depreciation to 31 March 1988	£6336
net book value before 1989 depreciation	£2564
1989 depreciation @ 20%	£513
total depreciation	£4500
	£500
	£5000

For the immediate 12 month period, an accurate estimate of depreciation is important (for budgetary purposes), which is why the above detail is necessary. (Note that for the forecasts the depreciation amounts have been rounded to the nearest £1000.) For the period 1990 to 1991, this need not be quite so accurate and we can use a simpler forecasting method, the relationship of sales to fixed assets (at net book value). In 1989, this relationship is as follows:

$$\frac{\text{Sales}}{\text{net book value of fixed assets}}$$

$$= \frac{£180000}{£15600}$$

$$= £11.54$$

Assuming a small increase in 1990 and 1991 to £12 and £12.50 respectively (from £10.61 in 1988 and £11.54 in 1989), fixed assets at net book value will be:

$$1990: \frac{£208800}{£12.00} = £17400$$

$$1991: \frac{£242200}{£12.50} = £19376 \text{ (rounded to £19400)}$$

(2) *Stock* is projected using the stock days ratio. Previously stock days went up from 25 to 39 days and we think that this is likely to be a permanent feature of trading in the future. Thus we shall project at 40 stock days:

$$1989: \quad \frac{£38700 \times 40}{365} = £4240$$

$$1990: \quad \frac{£43800 \times 40}{365} = £4800$$

$$1991: \quad \frac{£49600 \times 40}{365} = £5400$$

(3) *Debtors* are projected at 36 debtor days, which is in line with the trend (1988 was 40 days and 1987 was 36 days):

$$1989: \quad \frac{£180000 \times 36}{365} = £17800 \text{ (our cash flow forecast put debtors at £18000 – close enough)}$$

$$1990: \quad \frac{£208800 \times 36}{365} = £20600$$

$$1991: \quad \frac{£242200 \times 36}{365} = £23900$$

(4) *Cash* in 1989 has been set by the cash flow forecast. In 1990 and 1991 cash has yet to be determined and is, in fact, a balancing item. It can be left until last as it affects the amount of money needed to run the business (see section 11 below).

(5) *Creditors* follow a trend of 65 days payment established in previous years:

$$1989: \quad \frac{£38700 \times 65}{365} = £6900$$

$$1990: \quad \frac{£43800 \times 65}{365} = £7800$$

$$1991: \quad \frac{£49600 \times 65}{365} = £8800$$

(6) *Sundry creditors* includes VAT and PAYE payments (amongst others). The difficulty with this item is that it relates mainly to sales income but also includes a number of other creditor amounts, which

could vary from year to year. Therefore it is unlikely that any precise relationships could be established. The amounts seem to vary from 3.3 per cent of sales in 1987, to 4.1 per cent in 1988 and 5.2 per cent in 1989. The latter has been calculated from the cash flow forecast. If a figure of 5 per cent of sales is assumed (any differences are too small to bother about), projections of sundry creditors are:

$$1990. \ 5\% \times £208800 = £10400$$
$$1991: 5\% \times £242200 = £12100$$

(7) *Taxation* is taken from the profit and loss accounts for the respective years.

(8) *The overdraft* is projected to be nil in each of the three years. This does not deny the need for a facility to accommodate an overdrawn account *during* the year, but merely indicates that at the year end no overdraft is shown at the bank. The cash flow forecast for 1989 indicates that there should be cash in the bank account at the end of March. Cash and the overdraft are inversely related, of course, and the prime objective is to analyse financial requirements in order to identify short- and longer-term financial needs. At this point in the forecast, a nil overdraft is assumed.

(9) *Profit and loss* is brought forward from successive years' profit and loss accounts (after tax) into the balance sheets.

(10) *The bank loan* is assumed to be repaid at the rate of £1800 per annum.

(11) Returning to the question of a *balance*, Alcock's is now in a position to assess its financial needs over the three year planning period. Assuming a nil overdraft level (entered at the appropriate place) and an unknown level of cash in 1990 and 1991, the balance sheets can be completed as follows:

(a) completing the bottom section ('financed by' or sources of long-term finance), where all the necessary amounts now exist;
(b) calculating the *cash* or *overdraft* amounts by completing the arithmetic down to 'net assets'.

The purpose of forecasting the balance sheets is to identify the need for finance to meet working capital and fixed capital requirements. In section 11 above, cash, the overdraft and bank loan will have to be juggled to achieve an acceptable balance in terms of gearing and a matching of short- and long-term sources and applications of funds.

We have now completed the forecasts with a comprehensive set of sales, profit, cash and financial projections for a three year period. It has taken some time to get to this point, but there is no substitute for detailed planning and a considerable amount of learning has also occurred. This is one of the hidden benefits of corporate planning and financial forecasting. It is difficult to overstate the advance in personal knowledge that is manifested in the corporate planning process. And with the experience gained, next time the task will be that much simpler.

We have presented a comprehensive planning, forecasting and budgeting process in this chapter, starting with the sales forecast and finishing with detailed profit and loss accounts, balance sheets and cash flow forecasts. We can now move on to developing a use for the forecasts as a mechanism for monitoring and controlling business activity. For the benefit of the reader, we now bring together all the disparate elements of the corporate plan into a coherent whole. An 'exemplary' plan is provided in the following appendix.

Key points

- Planning ahead allows you to identify future business needs and take action before you are overtaken by events.
- All businesses should have a corporate or strategic plan and writing down the plan is an important discipline in ensuring that the direction you set is right and that your strategy stands up to rigorous examination.
- Objectives should be realistic and achievable in the planning period and should not conflict with one another.
- The SWOT analysis is a simple device for identifying what your strategy should be: build on your strengths and match them to opportunities.

- Accurate forecasting requires up-to-date historical accounts and records and a thorough understanding of future trends and factors affecting the prospects of the business.
- Cash flow forecasts should be based on the fundamental principle that income must not be overstated and outgoings must not be understated.

Appendix: Alcock's Joinery Limited: Corporate Plan April 1988–March 1991

Background

Alcock's was started in 1975 by Fred Alcock in a small workshop on an industrial estate in Lincoln. Fred Alcock was 33 at the time and had served his apprenticeship by the time he was 21. He was made redundant by his then employer who went into liquidation. By the mid-1980s Alcock's employed three skilled cabinet-makers and joiners and a part-time administrator and bookkeeper. Most of the selling was done by Fred Alcock. The company was regarded as rather old-fashioned but it had a good reputation for quality joinery and cabinet-making and had established itself as one of the city's better suppliers of individually designed fitted kitchens.

Objectives

To continue to improve net profit on sales to 8 per cent by 1991.
To build on a reputation for high quality joinery and cabinet making.
To grow steadily by no more than 16 per cent per year.
To reduce Fred Alcock's hours and subcontractors' time.

Strengths	*Weaknesses*
High-quality kitchens	Dependence on kitchens
Moderate pricing	Cramped space by 1990
Order book of 6 months	Shortage of apprentices
Excellent reputation locally	Unprofessional selling skills
Loyal workforce	Old-fashioned image
Good financial controls	Fred Alcock works too hard
Good relations with bank	Lack of internal information

Opportunities	*Threats*
Stand-alone furniture	High rents in alternative premises
Renovation of old housing	New joinery firm opened recently
Higher incomes	Saturation existing market by 1991
Main competitor closed down	Subcontractors closing down

Strategic choices

Products:	continue same range; modernize kitchens; commission designs for free-standing furniture
Production:	find new premises by 1990; renew lathe in 1989; find apprentice in 1989; reduce use of subcontractors
Marketing:	design brochure building on image and mail to select list; go on selling course; research furniture demand
Staff:	raise salaries; introduce bonus scheme; recruit
Management:	delegate more to Steve (foreman); manage time better; improve scheduling and planning
Finance:	raise profitability to fund furniture-making activity; review financing for new activities

Strategy

Alcock's will compete in its main market by offering local customers quality cabinet-making and joinery at modest prices and will test-market a newly designed range of furniture for domestic use in 1989. (See tables 4.2–4.8 as they are examples of the forecasts which should follow the strategy.)

5

Financial information for monitoring and control systems

Outline

Accurate information is the key to sound financial management. This chapter describes:

- the need for management information systems
- the different types of information small businesses need in order to make justifiable planning decisions
- how to record information
- how to implement control systems

If the purpose of business activity is to make a profit for the owners, it is in their interests to decide on the level of profit they require and whether the business remains small or grows to be large. Higher profit and lower risk generally provide a more comfortable and less stressed existence – the business owner has the difficult task of making decisions about profit and risk and balancing these against personal needs. The existence of *reliable and up to date information* will inform these decisions. In this chapter we shall examine the informational needs of a small business, identify the types of records that will provide the information required to make decisions, and describe the monitoring procedures and control systems that will keep the business firmly on course. Our aim here is to help you identify which records you should keep and enable you to set up a management information system, tailored to your own specific needs.

Management information systems

The use of financial, accounting, sales, production and other operating information for the day to day running of the business is called *management accounting* (as opposed to financial accounting which is accounting for historical performance). Effective management accounting requires information on a systematic and continuous basis if decisions about products, markets, production, people and finance are to be brought together into a coherent whole (the corporate plan) and the business is to achieve its profit objectives. The supply of regular continuous information is called a *management information system*. A system need not be computerized – it is a methodical and regular way of collecting, collating and using information for managing the business more effectively. Anyone can introduce and use an information system; there are, however, a few essential steps to be followed by the 'do-it-yourself' financial manager.

Management information has three uses:

(1) *As background information* for decision-making: it is often helpful to have a general picture of circumstances before progressing to the first planning stage. Indeed, being alerted to the need for control and planning decisions requires background information, even if the quality of the information presented is inadequate. The need to decide about salary reviews and promotion of individual members of staff, for instance, requires information about personal performance and individual contribution to company objectives. In many more ways the ingestion of general information about internal as well as external events is a necessary activity for the owner who wants to stay informed about problems and opportunities.

(2) *For forward planning* of the company's production, marketing, personnel and financial requirements: detailed planning and the production of accurate budgets requires a sound information base. We have seen in chapter 4 how historical financial information can be used to project profit and loss accounts, balance sheets and cash flow forecasts. The more accurate, detailed and up to date the information is, the clearer will the trends be revealed and therefore the more confident the forecaster will feel about the extrapolations.

Information needs for planning purposes are in two principal areas. The first is sales forecasting. Since sales forecasts are the origin of all financial projections, their importance cannot be over-emphasized. When forecasting sales, it is not enough to have detailed sales records over the past few years (although even this would be a bonus in some companies), since sudden changes in the marketplace can render history obsolete. The business needs detail about *very recent* sales effort (and rather less about previous years), a breakdown of sales leads and orders taken over the last six months, and a considerable amount of market intelligence about current and future trends, changes in buyer behaviour and competitor activity. Information in these areas comes from having an active *market research* capability.

Market research does not seem at first glance an appropriate subject for a financial book, but since the starting point for all business activity is having a *customer*, research into the needs of customers or potential customers has a high priority. Effective market research to gather information for planning purposes is undoubtedly best carried out while talking directly to customers and prospects because the quality of information is unadulterated and the researcher can explore people's perceptions and their likes and dislikes in an unobtrusive way. The 'researcher' in this case is anyone in the company who makes contact with the marketplace – it is *not* a person appointed solely to gather information.

Market information required for sales forecasting has financial consequences in four areas: the buying preferences of prospective customers will affect whether sales are made at all; the pattern of buying will affect the monthly distribution of unit sales; the magnitude of demand will affect the number of sales units forecast; the price per unit will affect the total value of sales forecast. The more relevant is the information gathered, the more accurate will be the forecasts.

A second area for active research is that of costs. Having established a projected level of sales which the market and the company can support, there is the question of the costs of making (production costs) and marketing the products or services (selling and distribution costs) and the costs of organizing and maintaining a base (administration and finance costs). Forecasts and budgets must take into account future costs (which could be based on historical costs) rather than last year's or current costs, because increases in costs are a fact of life and profit will be seriously eroded unless pricing allows for cost increases. Although we shall be taking a closer look at costing procedures later in this chapter, the basis of a reliable costing system is a knowledge of past and current costs and an informed view of future costs. These necessary requirements are the product of systematic information gathering.

(3) *For the purpose of monitoring performance and the effectiveness of financial controls*: pursuing the company's corporate plan and the general direction identified therein requires active management. Prospective deviations from the agreed strategy should be identified, investigated and killed off as quickly as possible, but more urgent are the inroads into profit and the drain on cash that result from departures from agreed plans and budgets, errors of judgement in decision-making and costing and pricing decisions on individual orders from customers. The latter are generally too late to correct but some action does have to be taken to stem the loss or cash flow drain. Whether or not the position can be reversed in the short term will depend on the individual business – it is not normally possible to make up lost profit or cash without a change in direction or a radical restructuring of pricing and financial controls, all of which need time to embed themselves.

Information needs for monitoring and control purposes follow a sequence:

1 Information is needed on a systematic basis to help identify areas where controls should be introduced in the first place or should be tightened up to improve performance. We need a way of identifying where problems are likely to occur and of generating information about the nature of these problems and their impact on the business.
2 Controls must be designed to deal with potential problem areas and to generate the necessary information flows that make the system work effectively.
3 In order to monitor *performance* and in particular profitability and cash, regular information is needed for monitoring purposes.

There are several principal characteristics of an effective information system:

1 Information should be *accurate* within acceptable limits. Since decisions will be made and plans drawn up on the basis of the information, its accuracy could have a significant effect on the outcomes. For example, it is important to know why your customers buy from you so you can gauge their sensitivity to changes in pricing, quality or delivery. If the information in your possession about customer behaviour is that they buy on price, then no amount of quality or delivery improvement will help.

2 Information is only useful when it is *complete*, because partial information could suffer from undue bias (particularly in the event of abnormal circumstances prevailing at the source of the information) and point to the wrong conclusions.

3 To ward off 'information overflow', only *relevant* information should be generated in the first place. Unnecessary information tends to cloud the issue under consideration and either slows up decision-making or results in errors of judgement.

4 Information should be *current*. Out of date information can be misleading, such as costs from last year's profit and loss accounts. Basing mark-ups or margins on these costs will certainly lead to under-pricing and lower profit.

5 The process of gathering, storing, retrieving and using information should be *cost effective*, in the sense of providing exactly what is needed at minimal cost. The costs of gathering usable information must be recouped from somewhere. If these costs cannot be recovered then there is some doubt that the information is worth gathering.

6 The information gathered should be *significant* in terms of its likely impact on decisions. Information of marginal use only is also unlikely to be cost effective.

7 It must be possible to *present* the information in a usable form. If the information is too complex to present in a practical way, it is unlikely to be understood by the user and therefore will be of no value.

Management information is required to ensure that the business is performing (in terms of profit) according to plan and will continue to do so, and that there will continue to be adequate cash to pay creditors in the short and longer terms. While *cash* is the lifeblood of the business, *profit* is the material with which a permanent presence is built, permitting the business to ride out the storms of market turbulence. A management information system is concerned principally with information that sheds light on the revenues and costs in the profit and loss account and the way that finance is used as shown in the balance sheet or cash flow forecast. Thus the business owner needs information about revenues, costs and financing methods in order to decide the following:

1 How to *maximize sales volume and income* through effective marketing. Decisions must be made about the marketing 'mix' – those factors affecting customers' buying decisions, such as which product, what price, what promotional methods and what channels to use. These decisions will require information about customer sensitivity to changes in product quality, the elasticity of demand to price rises, the profit margins associated with different channels of distribution and the cost effectiveness of different promotional methods. The first two are to be found in the marketplace (market research again) and the latter two inside the business.

2 How to *minimize variable costs of sales* (materials, stock, direct labour and subcontracting) through efficient production and effective purchasing. Up to date information about the costs of materials and stock from suppliers, industry wage rates and prices charged by subcontractors is a necessary condition for keeping production costs down; production methods need to be reviewed regularly and the appropriate method chosen to suit the requirements of customers, given the capacity constraints set by available production hours, space, machinery and technical considerations. The way that production is planned, organized, managed and controlled will also affect cost, and information will be needed on the latest production management methods. In a retail business, in order to contain stock levels to a minimum, the prime informational need is the availability of supplies at the right price and on the right terms.

3 How to *minimize fixed operating costs* through efficient use of resources and effective control of overheads. The owner has a number of important decisions to make about how to organize the administrative function, since the costs of administration, particularly rent and salaries, normally the largest fixed cost items in the profit and loss account, are difficult to allocate fairly to the different products and markets reached by the business.

4 How to *minimize the need for finance* through effective control of revenues and costs and of fixed and working capital. Unless the business is consistently profitable and has favourable trading terms (it receives its payments early or in advance), it is likely to require increasing amounts of short-term finance (the overdraft). Controlling this requirement is vital to long-term success and we return to this point in chapter 6. By effectively controlling costs while maintaining sales income levels, profit will be maximized and financing from external sources reduced. This in turn will help to keep finance charges (interest) under control, which will in turn affect profitability. Control of fixed and working capital, which we shall develop shortly, leads to a reduction in short- and long-term financing, which puts the business into a stronger position with its external providers of finance (usually the bank) and reduces interest and capital repayments and therefore improves cash flow.

An effective management information system should be designed for the specific needs of the individual business. There are well-established principles of design and in practice it would not be necessary to start from scratch. We describe some of the main elements of a control and monitoring system shortly, but for those businesses where there may be special informational needs, the following steps should be taken:

(1) A *review and analysis of business decisions* should be undertaken to identify their nature, frequency and timing. For instance, pricing policy requires information on the nature of the product lines being sold to a particular market segment, the contributions required from each line, the buying habits of customers in that market and the frequency and timing of their buying decisions.

(2) The *information requirements* at each decision point should then be analysed and noted, identifying whether the information would be collected from internal or external sources. On the sales side we would need to know a great deal about the customer and final consumer (age groups, disposable income, tastes, location, storage capacity, quantities etc.) and on the production side about costs, delivery times, production methods etc.

(3) Having established how the information is to be used and what types of information are required, we are now in a position to *design*

an information system to produce the information. There are three elements within this stage:

(a) Information must be *collected, collated and stored* in an appropriate way. Collection is arguably the greatest problem in most businesses since no formal procedure normally exists. This is not to say that information does not exist: it is usually present but needs organizing. Some of the highest-quality information is collected inadvertently by people who are constantly out in the marketplace talking to customers and competitors, keeping their ears close to the ground and their eyes peeled for signs of opportunity and change. The only question is how can all these valuable data be *recorded*? We return to this issue later. Once the information has been collected, someone should be responsible for sorting and assembling it (collation) into a usable format and storing it for later use. This could involve the use of a computerized database or a manual system. The choice will depend on the cost effectiveness of the information supplied under either method, which will largely depend on the frequency of use and the complexity of the information requiring processing. A manual system is unlikely to provide complex information rapidly, whereas a computerized system is unlikely to produce simple information cost effectively.

(b) Once stored, the information has to be *retrieved and processed*. In a manual system, this means setting up an appropriate recording and filing system to permit easy access. The right database program must be selected and, if a computerized system is preferred, the choice is not at all easy given the large number of databases on the market and their relative prices. Professional advice is recommended at this point and it would be wise to investigate more than one product.

(c) Finally, information has to be *presented and used* effectively. Clear and concise presentation, particularly if other people are involved in the decision-making, will help to get the right decisions made as quickly as possible.

Information requirements for small businesses

Information can be broken down into requirements which affect either day-to-day or long-term planning decisions. The former include the following:

Information affecting aggregate sales income and gross profit margin

Aggregate sales income is affected by the number of units sold and the average price per unit. Unit sales are primarily affected by the marketing mix. Price is an important consideration because higher prices not only increase sales value but also gross profit margin (other things being equal). Information that affects pricing decisions is vital. To make the right pricing decisions, information is needed about the *desired contribution* from each product or product range and from each customer or market segment. This is to be found in the business plans. In other words, if the average contribution required is known, to ensure a desired level of profit for the business as a whole, individual product contributions can be used to set prices. (Remember that 'contribution', or gross profit, means contribution to fixed costs and net profit.) Using aggregate gross profit margin as a guideline, margins can be examined and adjusted appropriately.

The adjustment process depends on customer reaction to price changes and the impact of competitors and other external influences. The desired gross profit margin may be untenable in a given competitive situation. Therefore you will need information about *customer sensitivity to price changes, what competitors are doing or about to do* and the likely *impact of environmental influences* (government, society). To inform decisions about these three areas, you will require up-to-date market intelligence about customers, competitors and government policies. Much of this can be gleaned through existing internal activities, specialist publications and the media, and so there should be little additional cost to the business of generating this information.

Gross profit margin is also affected by the variable costs of sales. Information about *factory operating costs*, *raw materials costs* and *direct labour costs* (or the cost of stocking the shop) is required for decision-making about pricing. Factory costs can be obtained from internal records. Information about labour and materials costs should be continually revised by periodic researching of local labour markets and suppliers. Internal records of wage rates and supplier prices should be adjusted accordingly. The costs of making or buying in individual products can be calculated from the aggregate cost structure described above.

Information affecting fixed costs

Marketing effort required to get potential customers interested in the product and then to buy it should account for a substantial proportion of total costs. Information on marketing expenditure as it affects sales should cover mainly *promotional and advertising activities*, although changes in *the costs of selling and distributing* could also affect sales and therefore should be monitored as well. The importance of collecting information on marketing activities lies in the nature of marketing costs, which are variable to a degree and are frequently direct in nature. This makes them allocable to specific products or markets and therefore their impact on sales can be observed and recorded.

The remaining fixed costs – *administration and financing costs* – must be recovered from gross profit. Because they provide support for the organization as a whole, regardless of sales or output, these fixed costs cannot easily be allocated to a product or customer other than arbitrarily. Information about them is required on an aggregate basis, therefore, but there is still every need to maintain proper records of expenditure in these areas.

The purchase of fixed assets and *depreciation* policy affect fixed costs. Information on the useful life, original cost and replacement rate of depreciation of assets will be needed for costing and pricing decisions. Depreciation is frequently omitted altogether from cost calculations, which can leave very little surplus for future purchases of fixed assets.

Recording information: bookkeeping and other source documents

The books of account form the main record of historical performance and are a valuable source of information about costs and revenues. As a secondary source they are rather less helpful, however, and we must go to primary source documents such as invoices, receipts and other records of production and sales for information about costs and revenues associated with specific products and markets.

Bookkeeping is at first glance an arcane activity; further examination reveals that it is common sense, particularly if it is tailored to the needs of the individual business.

A simple bookkeeping system

For the smallest business (with sales turnover up to £100000) a simple set of books of account and supporting records are adequate and will provide a record of all the information required in the business, as well as satisfy Inland Revenue requirements. A simple system can easily be operated manually; indeed there would be no point in computerizing the accounts if all the informational needs of the business could be provided by a simple system. (Because a full explanation of bookkeeping for the beginner requires a book of its own, the following section assumes some knowledge of bookkeeping and a willingness to explore further in other texts, or to discuss bookkeeping needs with a qualified accountant or professional bookkeeper.) A simple system comprises the following:

analysed cash book
petty cash book
daily takings book (for retailers only)
cheque stubs
paying in book
ring binder containing paid supplier invoices
ring binder containing paid customer invoices
creditors file
debtors file
petty cash box
petty cash envelope
bank statements file
VAT account

Analysed cash book

A cash book contains a chronological listing of payments (usually at the front of the book) and receipts (usually starting somewhere after the middle of the book). Note that we are concerned about *cash*, and so only *payments* out of and *receipts* into the business are accounted for in this book. The purpose of the cash book is to *monitor the current account at the bank*, so that the owner is kept informed on a daily basis about cash flow, which we have already identified as the lifeblood of the business.

An analysis of payments and receipts should be contained in the cash book by using the multi-column format found in all analysis books. On the payments side, column headings should include not only the date paid, payee, cheque number and total amount, but also a breakdown (analysis) of the payments as follows: input VAT, net amount paid and details of the payment under respective headings such as wages, rent, electricity, stationery, equipment, petty cash etc. A full list of headings can be taken from the profit and loss accounts discussed earlier, remembering not to include stock and depreciation (which are not cash entries). Be sure to include a 'miscellaneous' column for such payments as taxation and VAT and any other infrequent items not accounted for elsewhere, and a 'balance' column at the far right-hand side where the bank balance can be entered (see below).

On the receipts side, a common-sense arrangement would include date banked, payer, total amount, output VAT, net amount and further detail of the payment (although this is optional), broken down into type of customer (customer group), type of product and an 'other' category. There is no legislated format for the analysed cash book and the owner should use a common-sense approach to setting out an analysis which best suits the needs of the business.

For the self-employed where not much analysis is needed, it will be possible to enter the payments on the left-hand page and the receipts on the right-hand page, with a 'balance' column shown on the same page. In a business with more than one person (say sales income over £50000), payments and receipts should be kept up to date (or whenever a payment is made or cash banked) and the 'balance' column calculated daily. This is the only way that cash at the bank can be monitored accurately. At the end of the month, the bank statement would be reconciled with the balance in the cash book to provide a check on the accuracy of the books of account.

Pragmatism should prevail when it comes to keeping books of account. If you are not interested in the information for decision-making, then there is no need for detailed analysis. If you are serious about using the information from the book to manage the business more profitably, however, consider acquiring a book with at least 30 columns (they run beyond 30). This will provide adequate space for a proper analysis and will also help when the end of year accounts have to be prepared (which should keep the fees down). Keeping detailed books will assist the extraction process. Do not be afraid to write notes in the books: at the end of the year you will have forgotten what a particular payment was for and if it was an unusual one (such as a rent deposit or a refund) it could cause a problem when compiling the balance sheet. Therefore simply annotate the entry at the bottom of the page. Finally, there is an advantage in buying a loose-leaf system: not only does it have more columns than a fixed-page book, but it does allow pages to be moved around, additions to be made and pages to be scrapped (mistakes will happen!).

Petty cash book

A record should be kept of all petty cash payments and, where possible, receipts collected and stored. The purpose of a petty cash book is to provide evidence of small amounts of expenditure not detailed in the cash book and to act as a control on these amounts. A petty cash book (a small hard-covered exercise book will suffice) will contain several columns with headings showing total amount paid, input VAT, net amount paid and further analysis, to include details of payments, such as postage, travel, office supplies, catering etc. Like the cash book, there should be a 'miscellaneous' column and a 'balance' column recording both deposits into petty cash and the amount of cash remaining after deducting payments from the opening balance. This balance can be checked against the actual cash in the petty cash box (see below).

Daily takings book

Retailers should keep a daily record of receipts (takings) which should be read off the tills at a regular time each day, totalled and entered into the book for the day. These amounts will be totalled for the week and can be compared with the previous year's daily and weekly takings, as well as with targets for the current year. The purpose of the daily takings book is to monitor progress over the year against budget and to act as a check on cash taken at the tills by reconciling the amounts with cash banked. The special problem facing retailers is that they deal almost exclusively in cash, which is always difficult to control, for obvious reasons. Thus further controls on cash will be required which are beyond the scope of the books of account. We return to these later in the chapter.

Cheque stubs and paying in book

These often neglected sources of financial information are invaluable to the smaller business, particularly when the cash book is rudimentary or not updated regularly. It is advisable to record as much detail as possible in the cheque stubs (not only the date, payee and total amount paid, but also VAT and an approximate running balance at the bank. This should avoid overdrawing the account beyond the already agreed facility and will enable a quick check to be made of VAT owed to Customs and Excise well before payment is due. This will also help with financial control as it provides evidence of payments made and receipts banked in the event of a dispute.

Ring binders containing paid supplier invoices and customer invoices

As primary evidence of sales invoiced and supplies purchased, all invoices and receipts should be filed carefully in appropriate order, either after they have been paid or after they have been entered for payment in the appropriate books of account. The filing order is a matter of common sense. On the expenditure side, normally it would be best to file in invoice date or payment date order (which should coincide with cheque sequence). On the sales side, filing in sales invoice number order is best. It is optional to enter on the relevant invoice the payment date, cheque number and amount paid, all of which act as additional controls on payments and receipts in the event of a dispute.

Creditors file and debtors file

In a simple system the only way to identify unpaid invoices is to file them separately in a 'bills to be paid' file (or creditors file) and an 'unpaid customer invoices' file (or debtors file). When their turn for payment arrives, they are then transferred to the respective 'paid' ringbinders. This simple device allows for an easy review of debtors and creditors at the end of the month, which is one of the monitoring procedures we shall be discussing shortly.

Petty cash box and petty cash envelope

A sturdy metal petty cash box with a lock is required. There are two rules of handling petty cash. Petty cash should be controlled by one person only (with an understudy in cases of emergency) for security reasons, and money should never be taken out without a receipt or voucher for the exact amount being placed in the box. At the same time, an entry should be made in the petty cash book. At the end of the month, there should be a reconciliation between the box and the book, and the receipts and vouchers should be checked against the book, stapled together, labelled with the month in question and put into a large brown envelope with the other months of the same financial year. This procedure provides a ready record of all petty cash and can easily be checked if discrepancies arise.

Bank statements file

Monthly (or weekly) bank statements should be reconciled with the cash book and filed in a statements file. Monthly statements should include the last calendar day of the month to facilitate a reconciliation with the month's cash book entries.

127

VAT account

This need not be a separate book of account and is best included somewhere in the cash book (possibly towards the back of the book). A separate account must be kept of certain VAT information in order to complete the quarterly VAT return:

total outputs for the quarter from the cash book;
output VAT;
total inputs from the cash and petty cash book;
input VAT from the cash and petty cash book;
VAT payable to/refundable by Customs and Excise.

The principal disadvantage of a simple bookkeeping system based on the analysed cash book is twofold. There is no ready record of monthly *invoiced* sales and purchases, which is required for budgetary control purposes (see later) and for the annual profit and loss account. With a little effort the correct amounts can be calculated as follows (the calculation must exclude items *not* found in the profit and loss account, such as equipment purchased and loans repaid):

Aim: to produce invoiced sales and purchases figures from the analysed cash book
Computation: cash book receipts/payments for the month
add: petty cash spent in the month
less: creditors/debtors from previous month
add: creditors/debtors for current month
equals: sales/purchases figure for current month

There is also no ready record of amounts owed to individual suppliers or from individual customers, which is required for monitoring purposes and for producing the annual balance sheet. In a very small business this would not present a problem as reference could always be made to the cash book and unpaid invoices files. However, in a larger business, particularly where multiple invoicing in a month is the norm (either to customers or from suppliers) or where payments do not always match the amounts presented in an invoice (for quite legitimate reasons), the cash book system is inappropriate.

Calculation of VAT payments to or from the Department of

Customs and Excise can be problematical with a simple system. Under present regulations, businesses with an annual turnover of less than £250000 can elect to pay VAT on a cash basis, for which the cash-book-based system accounts quite comfortably. However, should the business have to pay VAT on an invoiced basis (which is obligatory with a turnover of more than £250000), the cash book system requires some manipulating in order to calculate input and output VAT on an invoiced basis. This should not take much time, but it does constitute another administrative burden for the small business.

The cash book system does have one great advantage: it is simple to set up and operate. Very little effort is required to keep the system up to date and it produces an adequate quality and volume of information for performance measurement and financial control purposes.

Double entry bookkeeping : a complex system

A full double entry bookkeeping system provides the more detailed informational needs of a business to enable performance to be measured accurately and the appropriate monitoring and control procedures to be implemented. 'Double entry' means that when a transaction is entered in a book of account, it creates both a credit and debit in the balance sheet: for example, when a sale is invoiced, there is an entry in the sales day book (which affects the profit and loss account in the balance sheet) and in the sales ledger (which affects debtors in the balance sheet), and when the customer pays the invoice, there is a balancing entry in the sales ledger (which eliminates the debtor in the balance sheet) and another in the cash book (which affects cash in the balance sheet). Because of the greater degree of complexity of this system, it is conducive to computerization and there is probably little point in setting up a full manual double entry system from scratch. Nevertheless, the principles are worth explaining, for even if a computerized system is to be installed, there should be an existing manual system in place already.

The major disadvantage of a cash book system is that it accounts only for cash. This deficiency is not inherent in a double entry system, which consists of the following:

sales day book
sales ledger
purchases day book
purchases ledger
cash book
petty cash book
nominal ledger
salaries/wages book
fixed assets register
loans register
VAT account
files (as for simple system)

Sales day book

In order to record sales invoiced in a month, a sales day book is needed, which is a chronological listing of all sales invoiced (whether or not money has been received for the sales). Actual monthly sales figures are required for monitoring progress against budgeted monthly sales income and, by adding up the monthly totals, will also give annual sales income in the profit and loss account. The day books permit some analysis of the entries: in this case, each entry should show date of invoice, payer, total amount, output VAT, net amount and an analysis of the sale by product and/ or customer group in whatever detail is necessary. The entry should also be referenced to the relevant entry in the sales ledger for control purposes.

Sales ledger

The sales ledger consists of a double entry listing for each month of sales invoiced (the same amount entered in the sales day book) and payments received from the customer (also entered in the cash book when received). The purpose of the ledger is to provide instant information about debtors – monies owed by individual customers. To do this, each customer has a separate page to itself in the sales ledger showing amounts invoiced and amounts paid, leaving a balance of monies still outstanding. Each entry is referenced to the appropriate entries in the sales day book and cash book.

Purchases day book

Like the sales day book, the purchases day book chronologically records all variable and overhead purchases in each month of the year and therefore provides an entry in the profit and loss account for each expenditure item. The book records amounts invoiced, not amounts paid, and contains a detailed analysis of each entry: date of transaction (which would include invoiced amounts as well as direct debits and standing orders), supplier, total amount of purchase, input VAT, net amount and an entry under one or more of the profit and loss account expenditure categories. The headings used in the analysis columns should correspond to those appearing in the profit and loss account and thus will vary according to individual business requirements. Entries should be referenced to corresponding entries in the purchases ledger and, if the purchases are direct costs, they could also be coded to identify them with the sale or product to which they relate. This information should be useful for control purposes and for costing and pricing reviews.

Purchases ledger

The purchases ledger consists of a double entry listing for each month of purchases (the same amount entered in the purchases day book) and payments made to suppliers (also entered in the cash book when paid). The purpose of the ledger is to provide instant information about creditors – monies owed to individual suppliers. To do this, each supplier has a separate page to itself in the purchases ledger showing amounts invoiced and amounts paid, leaving a balance of monies still outstanding. Each entry is referenced to the appropriate entries in the purchases day book and the cash book.

Cash book and petty cash book

Unlike the analysed cash book which forms the basis of the simple system, in this instance the cash book need not be analysed in detail, although a reference to the source of the entry is desirable. Because of this, the balance between receipts and payments can be contained on the same page. Column headings could include: date paid/

131

banked, payer/payee, cheque number (for payments), total amount of payments, analysis of payments (whether from purchases ledger, wages book, fixed assets register or loans register), total amount of receipts, analysis of receipts (whether from sales ledger or elsewhere) and bank balance. The petty cash book is the same as that described earlier.

Nominal ledger

In order to bring together the day books, ledgers and cash books, there should be a nominal ledger, which provides a summary of sales invoiced and invoices paid (from the sales ledger) giving total debtors, and a summary of invoices from and payments to suppliers brought together under expenditure headings (from the purchases ledger) giving total creditors. In summarizing the ledgers, there is an effective summary of the day books and cash book and a control of the main accounts in the business in order to produce a balance sheet.

Salaries and wages book

Ancillary to the purchases day book is the salaries and wages book, which provides details of gross remuneration to each employee on a weekly or monthly basis and includes PAYE, National Insurance, pension and any other deductions. The headings follow the deductions working sheets supplied by the local tax office with additions to include other appropriate deductions. The purpose of a separate salaries and wages book is to provide detail on gross and net payments to each employee and to facilitate the completion of end of year returns to the Inland Revenue.

Fixed assets register

This register is a listing of plant, equipment, machinery, tools and buildings by value at cost, showing monthly and annual depreciation and net book value. The purpose of the fixed assets register is to provide a record of assets owned and detail for monthly profit and loss accounts. The headings in the register cover date of purchase and description of the asset, useful life or annual rate of depreciation (and whether straight-line or reducing-balance) and monthly and annual depreciation in each year.

Loans register

If the business has loans or hire purchase outstanding (from whatever source), the principal sums and periodic repayments should be recorded in the loans register.

Other books of prime entry

Certain types of business may require special books, or a business may require special books for a specific purpose, such as a clearly identifiable and separate project. Autonomous business units, divisions or departments may under certain circumstances require separate books of account. At the heart of an effective bookkeeping system are the informational requirements of the business – the books should reflect these requirements at all times.

VAT account

Like the simple system, a separate VAT account must be maintained.

Various files

Like the simple system, receipts and documents will require filing in the usual way and can be adapted to individual circumstances.

General sources of financial information

The books of account form an important source of information about performance. However, they do not complete the informational picture and do little to inform the decision-maker about matters requiring immediate attention, such as pricing decisions. The business must look elsewhere for complementary information sources. Many of the latter are to be found in the following monitoring and control procedures:

Sales records

Detailed sales records either by *customer* or by *product* are an indispensable contributor to decision-making about marketing strategy, sales targets, product plans, production methods, pricing policy and sales and marketing methods. Records should cover the number and type of products sold, details of orders taken from customers, prices paid, discounts given, details of sales leads where orders did not materialize, how customers heard about the business, customer reaction to promotional and sales literature and any additional information that would be useful in analysing response and conversion rates. Sales records will also identify contribution rates (gross profit margins) made by individual product groups and market segments. The design of a sales information recording system is paramount in the planning activities of the business and should reflect the particular needs and operating methods of that business. Very little can be achieved without detailed sales information and every business owner should ensure that designing a system receives the highest priority.

Time sheets and job cards

In manufacturing and services operations, a proper record of materials, direct labour and other direct variable and overhead costs is required to enable accurate costings to be calculated and contribution rates to be assessed on each product (figure 5.1). The matching of actual to budgeted costs is an important monitoring procedure and can only be accomplished effectively if the discipline of keeping time and job sheets is strictly observed. This discipline must come from the top – the importance of accurate records of time and materials should be communicated to the entire workforce and their relevance demonstrated by way of example. Frequent reviews of *standard costs* should be undertaken to ensure that costings are based on the latest available information. Contribution rates by product group and market segment should be calculated and stored in costing records for use in later pricing decisions.

In manufacturing businesses, the design of a system to record cost information will depend on the needs of the individual firm and the organization of its production and marketing functions. In services

```
JOB CARD          NUMBER
QUANTITY:         CUSTOMER:
TYPE:             ORDER NO:
DESCRIPTION:      COMMENTS:
                  ORDER RECEIVED:
                  WORK COMMENCED:

MATERIALS                                          DATE
Item        Quantity    Value        Notes
_____|_____|_____|_____|_____
        |           |          |                |
_____|_____|_____|_____|_____
        |           |          |                |
_____|_____|_____|_____|_____
        |           |          |                |
_____|_____|_____|_____|_____
        |           |          |                |
_____|_____|_____|_____|_____


LABOUR
Action    Start   Finish   Time        Notes
_____|_____|_____|_____|_____|_____
        |       |        |       |                |
_____|_____|_____|_____|_____|_____
        |       |        |       |                |
_____|_____|_____|_____|_____|_____
        |       |        |       |                |
_____|_____|_____|_____|_____|_____
        |       |        |       |                |
_____|_____|_____|_____|_____|_____
        |       |        |       |                |
_____|_____|_____|_____|_____|_____


PACKING NOTE NO:              SHIPPED:
INVOICE NO:
INVOICE VALUE:      _____

COST: MATERIALS:    _____ ESTIMATE: MATERIALS:    _____
      LABOUR:       _____           LABOUR:       _____
      TOTAL:        _____           TOTAL:        _____
      GROSS PROFIT: ____ (  %)         GROSS PROFIT: ____ (  %)
```

Figure 5.1 Example of a job card

operations a system will have to take into account time spent by chargeable employees and the organization of the marketing function. In retailing the problem of job or product costing does not arise since the cost of merchandise from the supplier is already known and is the only variable cost in the calculation. In short, designing an appropriate cost information system is a matter for the individual firm. Most of the ground rules discussed at the beginning of this chapter should be helpful in achieving this, but professional advice would be a helpful adjunct to individual effort.

Competitors

Moving outside the business, a certain amount of financial information from competitors would help the planning process. Keeping records of competitors' products, prices and marketing effort will assist decisions about your own marketing activities. These records need not be detailed – indeed, simply filing competitors' sales literature and brochures might help when it comes to planning new products or changing prices.

Suppliers

The same theme should be pursued with suppliers. Records of existing suppliers' sales literature and price lists should be supplemented with similar information from alternative sources. Advance warning of impending price rises will help with the preparation of costings, and records of current supplier prices (which should be recorded on stock or order cards) will also help when orders are placed. The correct completion of purchase orders using pricing records will assist with the monitoring of costs.

Environment

Information having a bearing on financial decisions, such as anticipated domestic inflation and currency exchange rates with export markets, is readily available from external sources and should be recorded and stored on a regular basis. This type of record need only consist of newspaper cuttings or government statistical publications, but could prove to be invaluable for planning purposes.

Control systems and monitoring procedures

There are two principal areas for control, i.e. cash and profit. Generating the level of profit called for in the business plan and simultaneously keeping a check on the use of cash, allocating it in the right quantities to fixed and working capital, should ensure financial stability.

But how does an effective financial control system ensure that profit and cash objectives are met? The following example using Alcock's Joinery demonstrates the consequences for profit and cash of a controlled versus an uncontrolled business. In the profit and loss account and balance sheet shown in tables 5.1 and 5.2 we see the 1988 figures on the left-hand side and another set of 1988 figures on the right, *but this time it is a hypothetical situation based on applying a range of financial controls* which we shall discuss following the accounts. (The 'h' in the second column denotes hypothetical.)

What has happened to Alcock's under the regime of tighter financial controls? The evidence is quite clear: higher sales as a result of a price rise of 5 per cent, accompanied by cost savings on materials (buying more prudently), more efficient management of labour time and lower stock holdings, produces a higher gross profit margin. In addition, some savings on overheads including lower interest payments as a result of eliminating the overdraft results in a higher net profit margin and more than doubles profit after tax. This is transferred into the balance sheet, on which attention now focuses.

Taking better care of equipment (regular maintenance) eliminates the need for a new tool, and tighter stock and credit controls accompanied by purchase order controls reduces the need for fixed and working capital finance. This and the increased reserves release cash and eliminate the overdraft. The end result is that the business is financially more stable with higher profitability and cash reserves in the bank, an outcome of small improvements in key areas and more commitment to controlling the fixed and working capital needs of the business. These controls fall into two areas: controls on

Table 5.1 Alcock's Joinery Limited: profit and loss account for the year ending 31 March

	1988 £	1988(h) £	Change %	Control
Sales	154670	162403	+5	Regular costings
Less: cost of sales				
Materials	35290	34584	−2	Purchase orders
Opening stock and WIP	2130	2130		
	37420	36714		
Closing stock and WIP	3790	3316	−12	Stock control
	33630	33398		
Direct labour	46750	45815	−2	Time sheets
Subcontractors	9500	9500		
	89880	88713		
Gross profit	64790	73690	+14	[GPM: 42% to 45%]
Travel and motor	6653	6653		
Advertising	4218	4218		
Rent and rates	10500	10500		
Light and heat	808	808		
Insurance	560	560		
Repairs and maintenance	962	962		
Telephone	895	895		
Printing and stationery	1790	1590	−11	Budgetary control
Postage	679	679		
General expenses	846	846		
Audit and accountancy	795	795		
Salaries and NIC	20560	20560		
Bank interest	1410	1210	−16	[less borrowing]
Bank charges	378	378		
Depreciation	4640	4390	−5	See balance sheet
	55694	55054	−1	See above
Net profit	9096	18646	+105	[NPM: 5.9% to 11.5%]
Taxation	2445	4661		
Transferred to reserves	6651	13985	+110	

Table 5.2 Alcock's Joinery Limited: balance sheet at 31 March

	1988 £	1988(h) £	Change	Control
FIXED ASSETS				
Equipment and machinery	39760	38760	−£1000	Care of equipment
Motor vehicle	8900	8900		
	48660	47660		
Less: depreciation	34091	33841	−£250	Result of above
	14569	13819		
CURRENT ASSETS				
Stock and WIP	3790	3316	40>35d	Stock control
Debtors	16863	15573	40>35d	Credit control
Cash	3481	12283	+£8802	End result!
	24134	31172		
Less: CURRENT LIABILITIES				
Trade creditors	6285	5211	65>55d	Purchase orders
Sundry creditors	6295	6610		[4% of sales as before]
Taxation	2445	4661	+£2216	See profit and loss
Overdraft	2503	0	−£2503	End result!
	17528	16482		
NEW CURRENT ASSETS	6606	14690		
NEW ASSETS	21175	28509		
FINANCED BY				
Share capital	2000	2000		
Profit and loss account	11261	18595		[See profit and loss account]
	13261	20595		
Bank loan	7914	7914		
Capital employed	21175	28509		

revenues and costs (i.e. the profit and loss account) and controls on fixed and working capital (i.e. the balance sheet).

Controls on the profit and loss account

Budgetary control

Using monthly budgets as a means of control is the most effective method of monitoring performance on a regular basis and identifying potential problem areas. Budgetary (or variance) analysis provides a ready picture of actual income and expenditure in the most recent month and the year to date and compares each item with the budget. It is taken from the projected monthly profit and loss account (which we produced earlier) and laid out as shown in table 5.3 (we shall use Alcock's again).

What does budgetary analysis mean and how can it be used as a control device? The table is based on the monthly budgeted profit and loss account which we developed in chapter 4 (and so no additional work is required). The layout is a little different: the first three columns are entries for the current month (in this case June) and the last three for the year to date (the quarter April to June). In July 1989 there would be sufficient information to prepare table 5.3.

Having entered the budgeted figures for the month of June and for the year to date (by totalling the three months to June), we are now able to enter the *actuals* in the columns provided from the books of account. Starting at the top, we have the following entries.

Sales: from the sales day book for June (where the running total will also be shown)
Expenditure: from the purchases day book for June (where the running total will also be shown)
Stock: from stock control system or stock count
Depreciation: from the fixed assets register

The variances (expressed as $+/-$ in the columns) are calculated by subtracting the actuals from the budgets for each item. At a glance we have the company's performance up to date and action can be taken if necessary.

It is clear that Alcock's is performing worse than was originally forecast. There should have been a small net profit in June, whereas

Table 5.3 Alcock's Joinery Limited: budgetary analysis, April 1988–March 1989 (£ thousand)

	Month: June			Year to date		
	Budget	Actual	+/−	Budget	Actual	+/−
Sales	14.1	13.9	−0.2	24.7	22.7	−2.0
Materials	3.0	2.9	−0.1	5.4	5.2	−0.2
+Opening stock	3.9	3.9	0.0	3.9	3.9	0.0
−Closing stock	3.9	3.9	0.0	3.9	3.9	0.0
Direct labour	4.6	4.4	−0.2	13.8	13.5	−0.3
Subcontractors	0.7	0.7	0.0	1.9	1.9	0.0
Cost of sales	8.3	8.0	−0.3	21.1	20.6	−0.5
Gross profit	5.8	5.9	+0.1	3.6	2.1	−1.5
%	41.1	42.2		14.6	9.3	
Travel/motoring	0.6	0.7	+0.1	1.8	2.0	+0.2
Advertising	0.3	0.6	+0.3	0.9	1.4	+0.5
Rent/rates	1.0	1.0	0.0	3.0	3.0	0.0
Electricity	0.1	0.1	0.0	0.3	0.3	0.0
Insurance	0.0	0.0	0.0	0.1	0.2	+0.1
Repairs	0.1	0.3	+0.2	0.3	0.6	+0.3
Telephone	0.1	0.4	+0.3	0.2	0.6	+0.4
Printing/stationery	0.2	0.1	−0.1	0.4	0.2	−0.2
Postage	0.0	0.1	+0.1	0.1	0.2	+0.1
General	0.1	0.3	+0.2	0.3	0.6	+0.3
Accountancy/audit	0.1	0.1	0.0	0.3	0.3	0.0
Salaries	2.1	2.8	+0.7	6.3	7.4	+1.1
Interest	0.1	0.1	0.0	0.3	0.1	−0.2
Bank charges	0.1	0.1	0.0	0.1	0.1	0.0
Depreciation	0.4	0.4	0.0	1.2	1.2	0.0
Total expenses	5.3	7.1	+1.8	15.6	18.2	+2.6
Net profit/loss	0.5	(1.2)	−1.7	(12.0)	(16.1)	−4.1

there was a net loss of £1200. In all three months the company has been losing money at a greater rate than was budgeted (by £4100). Where do the problems lie and what can be done? An analysis of the variances shows that sales continues to be down on target, although given the seasonal nature of demand, the position is not irrecoverable (down by £200 on the month and £2000 on the three month period). Cost of sales is consequently down, although there appears to have been a small improvement in gross profit in June (up by 1.1 per cent) which is a good sign (cost of materials and labour utilization are being contained). Overheads are well over budget for June and for the year to date, particularly selling expenses (£400 and £700 respectively) and salaries (£1400 and £1900 respectively).

As a monitoring device, the budget/actual analysis is an invaluable tool in assessing performance and identifying problem areas. The difficulty is discovering the *real* causes of budgetary variances: it is all too easy to jump to conclusions and a great deal of further analysis and investigation of activities, expenditure levels and costings over the past few months will have to be undertaken. Therefore budgetary analysis can only identify the problem areas – it cannot reveal the causes.

Having investigated further, a course of action can be devised to correct the situation: sales will need boosting (without cutting prices) and certain overheads brought under control, if possible making savings over the next few months or ensuring that *budgets are rigidly adhered to* until the position has improved. This is the meaning of *control through budgets*: unless decision-makers adhere to agreed expenditure limits and do their utmost to achieve sales targets, there is no point in having budgets. At the same time, however, budgets can be restrictive and should be flexible, with sufficient discretion to exceed them *if good reason can be given*.

Flexible budgeting is a practical response to the ever-changing business environment. A budget set before the start of the year could be significantly out of date six months later, particularly if plans change markedly at short notice. Budgets should not be cast in stone; if a change in plans is forced on the business, then the budgetary process must be flexible enough to generate an entirely new set of figures, based on new circumstances. Keeping a watchful eye on these changes is the task of the business owner.

Although budgetary analysis is used primarily as a monitoring and control device within the business, it has another important use. As a source of information about the business, it can be used to inform other directors, key managers and staff about progress and, since each of these groups will have useful ideas about the resolution of problems from their own perspective, involving them in the analysis could prove to be enlightening and could be used as a means of building up teamwork and staff loyalty. This is a matter of discretion, however, because if the business is performing badly without there being any obvious cause, there is a risk that people who do not have the skill to interpret financial information will draw the wrong conclusions. This could be bad for staff morale. Finally, the budget/actuals could be used to inform the bank manager about progress and in so doing build a better relationship with the bank, which could pay off handsomely the next time the overdraft facility is negotiated. (We return to this point in the next chapter.)

Costing and pricing reviews

The use of job cards where actual expenditure is compared with budgeted or estimated expenditure is an important control in ensuring the right level of contribution from each product or job undertaken. This control should be supplemented by periodic reviews of costings and costing procedures to ensure that current estimates and prices are pitched at a level that returns the required contribution rates.

A complete understanding of the market in which the business operates, and particularly of the preferences and behaviour of customers, will lead to pricing according to what the market will bear. This can be a difficult level to determine, particularly if the seller has little or no experience of the customer. However, by establishing the costs of making and selling the product, at least the seller would be in a position to set prices in the knowledge that money would not be lost on any individual product, thereby increasing overall profitability.

The costs of making a product are composed of *variable costs* and *fixed costs*. Variable costs, such as materials, labour time and subcontracting, vary in direct proportion to the quantity sold (or produced). In other words, if output were to double, variable costs would double. Fixed (or overhead) costs do not vary in direct proportion to output. Some costs are semi-fixed, in that they vary a little, or part of the cost varies (such as electricity). The only way to decide on the nature of costs is to examine them carefully and observe their behaviour as output changes.

In order to set prices on the basis of total costs per unit of output, the following information is required:

$$\text{variable cost per unit}$$
$$+ \text{ fixed cost per unit}$$
$$= \text{ total cost per unit}$$
$$+ \text{ net profit per unit}$$
$$= \text{ price per unit}$$

This seems straightforward. For a single-product business where the production process is uniform, a simple costing procedure can be devised and applied with accuracy. However, in more complex businesses, the costing process requires considerable attention. The following costing explanations are based on, firstly, a simple business situation and, secondly, a more complex one:

(1) *Costing for a one-product business*
  Step 1: Calculate variable cost per unit.   Imagine for the sake of the exercise a small version of Alcock's Joinery where a single craftsman designs and makes furniture in a small workshop, employing one cabinet-maker to work on production. An order is taken for a piece of furniture which, with design, production and materials, would account for the following variable costs:

materials	£300
design time (30 hours @ £11.50 per hour)	£345
production time (120 hours @ £5.50 per hour)	£660
total variable costs	£1305

The first question arises over the hourly rates. How are these calculated? You need to know how many *productive hours* are available in a period: in this case, assume that the cabinet-maker works a 40 hour week at 80 per cent efficiency for £175 per week, which works out to be £5.46 per hour (rounded to £5.50). Design time can be similarly costed: the proprietor spends about 20 per cent of his time on design work, and if employed as a designer would earn £300 for a 35 hour week working at 75 per cent efficiency, or £11.43 per hour (rounded to £11.50). The fact that the design is done by the proprietor is immaterial. It should be costed in at an appropriate rate.
  Step 2: Calculate fixed cost per unit.   Now convert total fixed costs of £35670 (current year obtained from the budget) into unit fixed costs. The first task is to establish full production capacity in

terms of productive (chargeable) hours when operating normally:

cabinet-maker = 1440 hours per year (52 weeks less three weeks holiday entitlement, two weeks public holidays, two weeks sick-leave = 45 weeks @ 32 hours per week)

proprietor = 900 hours per year (50 per cent of time on design and production, based on 50 hours per week @ 80 per cent efficiency over 45 weeks)

total productive hours = 2340

Fixed costs (£35670) must be recovered from 2340 hours, giving an 'overhead recovery rate' of £15.24 per hour. Applying this rate to produce a unit fixed cost for each product based on estimated design and production time gives:

overhead recovery rate per hour	£15.24
productive hours (design and production)	× 150
total overhead recovery required	£2286.00

The overhead recovery rate is very specific to the business circumstances at the time. It suggests that fixed costs of £35670 would be recovered fully if 2340 hours were charged out. If either fixed costs or productive hours were to change, the recovery rate would have to change too. Thus the rate is very sensitive to changes in the two variables and constant reviews of overheads and productive hours are desirable.

Step 3: Calculate total cost per unit and pricing options. We can now summarize the costs so far:

variable costs	£1305
overhead costs	£2286
total costs	£3591

At a price of £3591 for the furniture, all costs would be recovered fully, but there would be no profit. Setting a price at an acceptable profit margin accounts for net profit in the following way:

desired net profit margin	=	10%
total cost (90%)	=	£3591
price (100%)	=	£3990

or

145

desired net profit margin = 20%
total cost (80%)   = £3591
price (100%)   = £4490 (rounded)

Pricing is a marketing issue and in the final analysis your customers will pay what they can afford. Knowing what this might be is an outcome of market knowledge, not of financial knowledge. But knowing what minimum price should be charged to either break even or make a desired level of profit, is greatly helped by adopting a logical approach to costing.

(2) *Costing for a multi-product business*

The problems of costing are multiplied for a more complex business. Not only are there different production processes, but there are different overhead allocations because certain overheads are directly related to a particular sale (and therefore output). The following example is based on a small electronics company called Doncaster Electronics Limited. In the current year (1989) the directors are trying to raise the gross profit margin from 35 to 38 per cent in order to raise net profits to 6 per cent of sales. Sales income is targeted at £1.8m with sales and distribution costs estimated at £108000 (6 per cent of sales), administration overheads at £450000 (25 per cent of sales) and finance and depreciation costs at £18000 (1 per cent of sales).

Since this is a manufacturing operation, gross margin is measured after variables and *direct factory overheads*, such as machine costs. There are two salesmen (paid the same salaries) who call on large companies in defence contracting and electronic engineering.

The company is asked to quote for two jobs (Jobs A and B) which entail producing a component for a large piece of electronic equipment. The component is a one-off, but a number of similar pieces of equipment have been produced before. The following information is available for Job A:

Estimated production time = 140 man hours + 60 machine hours

Engineers' time £5 per hour (salary of £10400 per annum)

Estimated materials costs including wastage £3200

Machine leased for £3750 per annum

Machine usage 1000 hours per annum

Estimated machine maintenance costs £1500 per annum

Sales takes five days of a salesman's time (out of 230 days)

Salesman's salary (including all on-costs) £25000 per annum

Sales conversion rate 2:1 on this type of work

The information on Job B is as follows:

Similar to Job A but a small amount of additional work is required, amounting to 10 hours of an engineer's time, 20 machine hours and £100 of materials. This type of sale is negotiated over the telephone (about half a day's work) and the customer always goes ahead, as it is a 'rush job'.

The costings will depend on the costing method used. If we adopt the overhead recovery method used in the single-product system, the fixed costs to be recovered in a full year are as follows:

selling costs	£108000
administration costs	£450000
finance costs	£ 18000
total fixed costs	£576000

Total number of productive hours in a full year:

Number of engineers	40	
Working hours per week	37.5	
Number of weeks per year	45	(52−7 for holidays etc.)
Total productive hours	67500	
@ 80% efficiency	54000	
Overhead recovery rate:	£576000	
	54000	= £10.67 per hour

Using this rate to cost jobs A and B:

	Job A	Job B
Overhead recovery	140 × £10.91	150 × £10.91
	= £1527	= £1637
	£	£
Materials	3200	3300
Direct labour	700	750
	3900	4050

Factory overhead		
Machinery: leasing	225	300
Maintenance	90	120
	315	420
Total direct costs	4215	4470
Overhead recovery	1527	1637
Total costs	5742 (94%)	6107 (94%)
Selling price (min)	6108 (100%)	6497 (100%)

What the company finally sells at will depend on their knowledge of the market. They should charge at least £6108 for Job A and £6497 for Job B if all variable and fixed costs are to be recovered and a net profit margin of 6 per cent achieved. While this is satisfactory from the point of view of simplicity and of recovering overhead costs, it does not differentiate among various direct overheads, such as selling costs, which appear to differ between the jobs. This distorts the profitability of individual jobs, results in some jobs losing money (because they do not recover their true direct overheads) and leads to a misallocation of resources in the company. An alternative method is needed.

A costing method that accounts for differential overhead allocation and ensures that profits are made on each job is as follows:

	Job A	**Job B**
	£	£
Materials	3200	3300
Direct labour	700	750
	3900	4050
Factory overhead		
Machinery: leasing	225	300
Maintenance	90	120
	315	420
Total direct costs	4215	4470

So far the costing is exactly the same as the previous method. But now a different approach is taken, using 'contribution' as a costing method. Although the business needs a gross profit margin of 38 per cent overall, it really needs a lower margin once direct selling costs, which include the salesman's time, have been taken into account. This reduced contribution rate should be calculated by looking at the business as a whole and in particular at the selling costs:

DONCASTER ELECTRONICS LTD
OUTLINE BUDGET 1989

	£	
Sales	1800000	(100%)
Cost of sales	1116000	(62%)
Gross profit	684000	(38%)
Selling		
Salaries	50000	(2.8%)
Other	58000	(3.2%)
	108000	(6%)
Administration	450000	(25%)
Finance	18000	(1%)
	576000	
Net profit	108000	(6%)

The contribution rate after accounting for cost of sales is 38 per cent. In other words, if you wish to set a price using this margin then the calculation is as follows:

	Job A		Job B	
	£		£	
Total direct costs	4215	(62%)	4470	(62%)
Selling price (min)	6798	(100%)	7210	(100%)

The problem with this approach is that it allocates the overheads on an equal basis and does not recognize that selling costs (the salesman's time) differ between the two jobs. Thus Job A (which takes more time to achieve the sale) could lose money if you were to allocate the due selling costs to it. You need another approach which allocates direct selling costs to each job first, and then applies a contribution to cover all *indirect* overheads.

149

	Job A		Job B	
	£		£	
Direct costs	4215	(62%)	4470	(62%)
Direct selling costs				
Salaries	1087	(2.8%)	54	(2.8%)
Total direct costs	5302	(64.8%)	4524	(64.8%)
Selling price (min)	8182	(100%)	6981	(100%)

This costing method permits the proper allocation of direct costs and the sharing of indirect costs. The result is that Job A is priced higher than under the previous costing method (£8182 versus £6798) while Job B is priced lower (£6981 versus £7210). This reflects the true direct overhead allocation and is a fairer method. Under the previous method, Job A appeared to be as profitable as Job B at a lower price, and vice versa. If the jobs were priced on this basis, the company would *lose money on Job A (which is under-priced) and might lose the order on Job B (which is over-priced)*.

It might be appropriate to allocate indirect costs in a different way, however, depending on the nature of the business. It is up to the management to develop the best costing methods for each situation. For instance, it would be appropriate to allocate other factory overheads (not just machine costs), such as rent, rates, building repairs, building insurance and cleaning costs, to each machine and work out a machine direct charge-out rate per hour. This can easily be done with the right information.

Controls on the balance sheet

Balance sheet controls are designed to minimize cash requirements, although there are incidental consequences for profitability. Any action that results in lower costs or higher revenues will affect profit as well as cash. We are principally interested in cash in this section, but will note in passing the impact of controls on profit.

Controls on fixed capital

There are two primary ways to control the growth of fixed capital: to take care of existing fixed assets so they do not have to be replaced before their useful life expires (or after, if possible), and to take possession of and use assets required in the business without purchasing them at all, or finance them without having to pay the full purchase price immediately.

(1) *Care of existing fixed assets*: by depreciating fixed assets over their useful life, an allowance towards replacing them is made against profit. The rate of depreciation, which is based on their useful life also reflects the company's policy on care and maintenance of assets. Longer life means a lower rate of depreciation (in theory) and therefore higher profitability. Since conservatism is a guiding principle in the preparation of accounts, it is normal to depreciate assets at a higher rate than reality might dictate, but this should not obscure the fact that the business will gain by not replacing assets until it becomes really necessary. There are several actions that can be taken to ensure that assets are replaced at the right time: there should be a company policy on the care and maintenance of equipment, tools, machinery, buildings and motor vehicles and the attention of all employees should be drawn to this policy; it would be prudent to designate someone to ensure that the policy is adhered to; employees should have a clause in their contracts of employment which obligates them to look after company assets; drivers of company vehicles should sign a vehicle care document (this is particularly recommended for sales people); users of specific items of equipment (such as computers) should have their attention drawn to correct operating and maintenance procedures; equipment and vehicles should be stored correctly when not in use; maintenance of equipment and regular servicing of vehicles should be costed into the company's budgets.

(2) *Use and ownership of assets*: a far more fundamental question is whether the business should *own* the assets (and therefore have to finance them) or simply *have the use* of them (and therefore not have to finance them). Ownership of certain assets is inevitable because it is not realistic to hire or lease them. But many others can be hired on a short-term basis (no finance required), hire-purchased over a period of time (finance spread over the period), leased (no finance required) or contract rented (mainly for vehicles where no finance is required). These options reduce the need for finance and there are sound arguments for using them. We shall examine them in chapter 6.

Controls on working capital

The financing of working capital has proved to be one of the greatest obstacles to successful growth of small businesses. The reasons are quite straightforward: working capital, unlike its counterpart fixed capital, cannot easily be seen (it has no unitary physical presence) and in the hurly-burly of managing the growing business (or bolstering the declining one) is normally forgotten or inadequately supervised. The end result is that growth in working capital exceeds the company's ability to finance it, there are severe cash flow problems, creditors call in their debts and the company is forced to capitulate. A few simple monitoring procedures and controls on working capital should ensure that potential problems are quickly identified and dealt with appropriately. We shall discuss these procedures and controls in logical order: stock control, credit control, cash management and purchasing control.

(1) *Stock control*: since only manufacturing and retail businesses carry stock, this section will not be of much interest to the service sector. Controls on the level of stock held in the business are designed to achieve two things simultaneously: to reduce the costs of holding and managing stock, and to reduce the amount of finance tied up. There are several types of cost: the financing of stock attracts interest charges; there are the costs of storage, both in terms of physical space (rent) and people to manage it (salaries); insurance can be an expensive item; there are administration costs (salaries again and data handling); there are the risks associated with fashion merchandise where the value could erode rapidly; and there is the possibility of damage to and pilferage of stock.

The object of stock control is to carry a level and range of stock that matches requirements for meeting orders while having sufficient buffer until new deliveries arrive. Information needed to decide on the right stock level and design an appropriate control system is as follows:

> current stock level in units;
> expected sales in units in the period ahead;
> minimum stock level required;
> re-order lead times;
> stock holding capacity.

Designing a stock control system means keeping the right level of stock and re-ordering just enough to meet the needs of customers in the next period, with a little in hand in the event of extraordinary sales. A manual system that facilitates re-ordering could be based on stock control cards, as shown in table 5.4. This stock control card is packed with useful and readily available information. All the ordering information is in front of the person placing the order, including supplier contacts, costs and delivery times. These should be verified when calling through the order but will help in planning the scheduling of orders. There could be a large number of items to order across a wide range of products from several suppliers (particularly in retailing), and a schedule showing which supplier to call, and when, would be invaluable in planning the workload in the month or week.

Table 5.4 Stock control card*

Item: 3″ wood screws	Supplier: Colliers Ltd
Unit: 50	Address: 13 Heat Street N8
Supplier Code: WS1093	Telephone: 01–356 4829
Minimum order: 100	Sales contact: Jane Jones
Delivery day: Thursday	Accounts: Sarah Wilson
Order by: Tuesday 12 noon	Terms: 30 days
Minimum stock: 200	Discount: 2.5% over £50
Cost: £1.24 Date: 1/1/89	
Cost: £1.36 Date: 1/8/89	
Cost: Date:	

	JAN	FEB
Date	4/1	6/2
Opening stock	200	280
Forecast sales for period	350	250
Forecast closing stock	200	200
Order (units)	350	200
Order (value)	£9.52	£5.44
Order date	5/1	8/2
Delivery (units)	350	200
Delivery (value)	£9.52	£5.44
Delivery date	7/1	8/2
Actual closing stock	280	50
Sales (units)	270	430

* This card should continue on from February to include all months up to and including December.

The order card identifies the minimum stock level required (possibly the minimum to fill a shelf with a small reserve) and the forecasts of closing stock levels and sales in the next period lead to a simple calculation of the number to be ordered:

orders = forecast sales + forecast closing stock − current opening stock

The principles of stock management form an integral part of stock control procedures and include the following: order only what the business needs and do not be deflected by 'special offers', no matter how tempting (stock rooms all over the world are full of special offers for which there is no demand); keep stock to a minimum, in line with sales and delivery lead times; store stock on or in appropriate storage or shelving systems and use it in strict rotation, drawing older before recently delivered stock (this is called 'fifo', or first in, first out); clearly label and price stock from the most recent price lists; count stock at regular intervals (monthly or quarterly) to check control card records and calculate 'shrinkage' − the amount of stock lost through damage, theft or error; enforce a strict code of practice when deliveries are received, checking quantities and condition before signing for them.

The monitoring of stock levels should include a monthly review of the stock days ratio (see chapter 3) and appropriate action taken if stock levels exceed planned levels. This will only reveal whether total stock holding is excessive and not levels of individual lines. Reliance should be placed on maintaining stock control cards for individual lines which can be set up and operated manually. In a small business it would not be cost effective to computerize stock records and ordering processes. As the business grows and the number of product lines expands, computerizing the records and ordering process will become increasingly necessary and more cost effective. The process of computerization is itself very time consuming and is unlikely to produce savings for some time. It certainly needs very careful consideration since it is not a decision that can be reversed easily.

(2) *Credit control*: the uncontrolled growth of credit to customers is potentially a most destructive force. Businesses frequently grant credit facilities without any questions asked and are then surprised when their customers cannot pay. People normally seem pleasant,

honest and financially sound enough when they apply for credit, but often this camouflages a more fundamental instability in their own businesses, which they either do not recognize or do not wish to reveal. The point is that customers do not normally set out deliberately to defraud their suppliers (there is a great deal of reciprocity in the buyer/seller relationship) and their inability to pay their bills is more often than not a reflection of their own inadequate marketing and financial management skills.

There are two potential problems with debtors: the more serious is that customers could purchase and consume a supplier's service without ever paying for it, because they cease to trade without leaving any assets to cover outstanding liabilities or because there is some dispute about the provision in the first place; the less serious but potentially equally damaging is the length of time that debtors are outstanding, because the customer cannot pay on time, there is a dispute about the invoice or there is no incentive to pay on time anyway. Let us now examine each of these problems in turn, demonstrating how monitoring and control systems can be used to reduce and eliminate problems with debtors.

(a) *Trade references*: it is standard practice in business to ask for at least two trade references from new customers. It would be foolish, however, to require a household name to provide references, even if they were thought to be a slow payer. Therefore taking trade (and bank) references is reserved for mainly smaller companies and certain larger ones where there could be some doubt about their creditworthiness. It is up to the supplier to contact these references and make enquiries about the customer's creditworthiness, asking questions about the amount of credit given, the customer's record in paying their bills on time and any problems that have arisen. Since it is unlikely that you will be given a disgruntled supplier's name, it would be wise not to place too much reliance on this credit check. If the references are positive, then take them for what they are worth: that the customer does pay at least some of its suppliers on time.

(b) *Bank reference*: there is very little a bank reference can achieve except to verify the customer's business name, establish that a bank account exists and that an agreed amount of credit per month could be met. This itself might be sufficient, however, and would help generally to establish a customer's credibility. The reference is taken by asking your bank to request a reference from your customer's bank.

(c) *Credit reference agencies*: checking your customer's credit-worthiness with a credit reference agency will inform you about any history of defaults and the credit rating of the customer. The weakness of using an agency is that the most untrustworthy businesses are either too small or too elusive to be included in the records. Unincorporated businesses are generally not included in agencies' credit records. Since the agency charges for this service, the costs must be related to the amount of potential debt being incurred – normally credit reports are worthwhile for large amounts or regular customers.

(d) *Agreeing credit limits*: before agreeing to supply the customer, you should agree a monthly credit limit. If there are no reliable references (particularly if the company is new or very small), it would be wise to extend only a very small amount of credit or preferably, if the customer agrees, to request cash with order until a relationship can be built up. By monitoring each customer's account very carefully (the sales ledger will reveal exactly how much credit each customer has taken, and is one of the main reasons for having a full set of books rather than a 'simple' set), there should be ample warning of any imminent over-running of the agreed credit limit.

(e) *Agreeing trading terms*: one common reason for late payment (or non-payment) is that the customer is in dispute with the supplier about the goods or services supplied, or about the invoice. Often a dispute arises because the terms and conditions of the sale are not made clear before the sale is closed. Minimum terms should be established and agreed in writing between the parties so that there is clarity on both sides. Naturally commercial law provides a framework with which commercial transactions must conform (such as the Sale of Goods Act) and the purchaser will have certain rights. To avoid expensive litigation, however, suppliers should minimize the possibility of disputes arising by persuading the customer to agree to certain basic conditions: an agreed maximum credit period by which payment must be received in full, the amount of discounts and under what conditions they may be taken, late payment penalties (it is unlikely that the courts will enforce these unless they are expressly agreed to before the sale is concluded), when the transfer of ownership is effected between the seller and the buyer (the so-called Romalpa clause whereby beneficial ownership does not pass until full payment is received), what form arbitration should take in the event of a dispute arising and other more specific conditions suited to certain industries. These and other terms should be set out clearly in advance of the sale (and signed by both parties), and noted on the invoice for the customer's benefit.

(f) *Invoicing procedures*: a sequence of sending delivery notes (if relevant), invoices and statements (if relevant) should be adhered to strictly in order to simplify the presentation of bills for payment and to ensure that all amounts sold and delivered are actually charged to the customer. If there are frequent deliveries of goods, a delivery note is essential to confirm that delivery has taken place and that the customer has received the delivery in good condition. A statement of account is required when there are several invoices in a period (a month) to ensure that the customer pays all due invoices on time. The invoice should contain the following information (figure 5.2):

Supplier's name and address, telephone number, fax number, telex number, VAT number, invoice number, contact name;

Customer's name, address, order number, account number;

Date of invoice (tax point), delivery note number, quantity delivered, product code, unit price, total price, VAT, discounts applied, net price, payment date, Romalpa clause, penalty clause.

(g) *Insuring bad debts*: another method of minimizing the financial cost of bad debts is to insure invoiced sales against the debt going bad. Bad debt insurance can be quite expensive but could be used selectively for larger or more risky sales. Included here would be sales to foreign customers, where a comprehensive package of financial and other trading assistance should be sought.

(h) *Procedures for chasing doubtful and slow debts*: there are as many methods of tackling slow payers as there are slow payers themselves and everyone will have their favourite. Having ensured that no disputes can arise about the goods delivered by implementing all the controls mentioned above, in the event of a debt showing no signs of being paid, the following are generally accepted approaches to collecting debts. The first question to settle is whether there is a dispute or not and indeed whether the customer actually received the invoice. The use of heavy legal or other threats at this stage is

ALCOCK'S JOINERY LTD
15 Short Street
Lincoln
Lincs LE1 8RD

Tel: 02367 5674
VAT REG. No. 238 9940 346 **Invoice**

INVOICE TO:

DELIVER TO:

INVOICE No:
TP/INVOICE DATE:
CUSTOMER REF:
PART/COMPLETE:
ACCOUNT No:

ITEM	STOCK NUMBER	DESCRIPTION	QUANTITY	PRICE	PER	DISCOUNT PRICE	AMOUNT

GOODS		VAT 15%	AMOUNT DUE

Notes:

PLEASE NOTE: Payment of this invoice is due to be received by us no later than 30th of the month following month of supply, unless other terms have been agreed.
Beneficial ownership does not change until full payment received.

If payment is received by as agreed, and account has been cleared up to date, please deduct the following discount.

Figure 5.2 Example of an invoice

bound to prolong payment and the best approach is to give the customer the benefit of the doubt with an enquiring telephone call to establish whether there is a problem. If this is not the case and no satisfactory explanation is forthcoming, it could be worthwhile offering to call immediately to collect a cheque. This direct approach often works well; otherwise you should set a time limit for payment. If this fails and there is no prospect of collecting the debt without some kind of legal action, then you will have to decide whether the reward is worth the likely costs, bearing in mind that there is no certainty that you will have the costs of the action awarded against the defendant if you win. One way of deciding is to take a view on the customer's willingness to enter into a protracted court case and the bad publicity that would almost certainly result. The larger the customer, the more likely it is that you will end up paying out more to pursue your rights than you would wish and the more damaging this would be financially.

There are several solutions to the problem of costs. You could design a procedure that automatically comes into effect when a bill is late for payment, starting with a strong letter and ending with a threat to take the customer to court. This approach has the disadvantage (as with all procedures) that the customer could call your bluff. The small claims court provides an alternative option: you can request a hearing and there is no need to employ a professional to act for you. Costs are minimal and claims of up to £5000 can be heard in the County Court. Where the amount claimed is less than £500, the court can refer the action to arbitration. This process can be time consuming and there is no guarantee that, even if judgement is entered against the defendant, you will ever be paid. A third option is to use professional debt collectors who work on a commission basis. A final option is to pass the responsibility of collecting debts to a factoring company, which will manage your sales ledger and collect any slow or doubtful debts on your behalf. (We shall discuss factoring in chapter 6.)

(i) *Monitoring debtors*: at the end of every month when the monthly budget/actual analysis is prepared, a list of debtors should also be prepared, aged individually and in aggregate, and the potential problem payers identified as early as possible for action. Action should not only include the follow-up procedures described above, but most importantly you should review the customer's current credit limit and consideration should be given to withdrawing supply immediately.

In the final analysis, you will have to consider whether the bad feeling engendered by continual badgering of slow payers is worth the potential reward. At some point you will decide that it is not worth having customers who pay late and who cause you endless grief. The costs of chasing them up start to affect other parts of the business. At this point it would be prudent to 'bite the bullet' and write off the worst cases.

(3) *Treasury management*: managing the balance between cash surpluses and deficits constitutes the treasury function. Efficient cash management should minimize interest payments to the bank and maximize interest received when monies are on deposit. This is achieved through two actions: diligent cash flow forecasting on a regular basis, which allows the planning of borrowing requirements well in advance of additional cash being needed, and the monitoring of cash balances on current accounts through the cash book, kept up to date on a daily basis. The effective use of surplus cash by investing it wisely either in additional fixed assets (such as a building) or outside the business requires a thorough knowledge of the rewards from alternative investment opportunities.

(4) *Purchasing control*: the monitoring and control of creditors is the final area for increasing profit and containing the amount of finance needed in the short term. Creditors (suppliers) are a valuable source of short-term finance through the credit negotiated with them. It is in your interest to maximize the amount of credit you can obtain, within reason, since you have a reciprocal relationship with your suppliers: taking undue credit is likely to disturb any good relationship that exists.

Other than maximizing the amount of credit offered by suppliers without upsetting them, there are several additional measures that will help to keep costs under control. Supplier selection is the first. When selecting new suppliers, particularly when the selection is strategically important, it is advisable to 'shop around', discussing availability, credit and delivery terms, and prices. Negotiating favourable terms can bring considerable additional benefits, and suppliers are often prepared to offer quite substantial discounts or special credit and delivery terms to win new business. In certain cases it would be prudent to practise multiple sourcing, even if this does mean giving up a small cost advantage.

Instituting appropriate ordering procedures should be a priority as the business grows and the owner is no longer able to exercise close personal supervision of purchasing. *Purchase orders* should form the backbone of creditor control: a purchase order with sequential numbering should be produced every time an order is placed, together with the signature of the person authorized to approve purchases. It would be wise to have at least two people in the business with this authority. The purchase order form (figure 5.3) should contain the following information: business name, address, telephone number, VAT number, purchase order number, date of purchase, date of expected delivery, supplier's name and address, details of purchase (number of units, description, price, total amount), terms offered, delivery note number (if any) and a space for the authorized signature. Once the delivery is received, the delivery note should be filed with the purchase order, matched with the invoice when received and finally checked against the monthly statement. This procedure ensures that only those goods and services ordered and delivered are actually paid for, and at the right price.

Once this system is in operation, payment procedures are quite straightforward. Every statement or invoice should have a matching purchase order and delivery note – thus nothing is paid in error. Exceptions can be made for payments where a purchase order is superfluous, i.e. for regular payments such as leasing or bank charges. Payments should always be by cheque, except in the case of petty cash expenditure, because they generate their own record automatically: the cheque stub is a highly effective monitoring device and is inexpensive too!

This completes our tour through the monitoring and control procedures to be found in the well-informed and tightly controlled business. Comprehensive information systems and controls will certainly help to identify potential problem areas before they become irretrievable. A basic information system should report monthly with the following, made up to the last day of the previous month:

1 budget/actual analysis, highlighting problem areas and possible causes of variances;

PURCHASE ORDER

Alcock's Joinery Ltd
15 Short Street
Lincoln
Lincs LE1 8RD

VAT Reg. No. 238 9940 346

Supplier

Purchase Order No.
1486

Purchase Order Date

Delivery Date

Quantity	Goods	Unit Price	Discount Price	Amount
			TOTAL	

TERMS

Authorised: Del. Note. No. Inv. No.

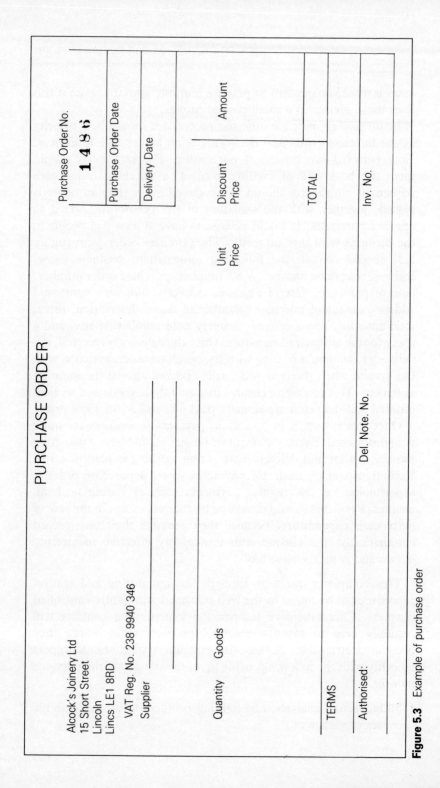

Figure 5.3 Example of purchase order

2 cash position at the bank (on all accounts);
3 list of individually aged debtors, plus total debtors;
4 list of individual and total creditors;
5 stock value, with identified problem lines.

In a competitive market, a business needs to be well informed and tightly controlled to ensure that it achieves the maximum gross profit margin possible, while keeping fixed costs to an acceptable minimum. We have explored the information and control systems needed to produce the required level of profit – you should now review your own systems and procedures, starting with the key question: 'What information is needed to make the right business decisions?' Needless to say, effective financial management may achieve stability in the short term, but at the end of the day business success is based on an arcane chemistry of marketing, finance and people. Having adequate finance to make this chemistry work profitably is the subject for discussion in the final chapter. We turn now to the thorny (and inevitable) matter of raising finance.

Key points

- Your business should have a system for providing up-to-date management information in order that the decisions you make are both effective and timely.
- Information is needed on the external environment, particularly about markets and the behaviour of customers, but also on the internal operations of the business, particularly the way in which costs behave in relation to sales.
- A simple cash book system is normally adequate for a new business, but rarely does it produce the necessary information for an established one.
- Budgetary control (monitoring actual sales and expenditure against budgets) is an indispensable tool in identifying potential problem areas at an early stage.
- Regular costings will ensure that prices charged properly reflect desired profit margins, but they require a considerable investment of time in designing a system that produces accurate data at the right time.
- Tightening-up controls and procedures on working capital (stock, debtors and creditors) will release much-needed finance into the business.

6

Raising finance

Outline

Businesses need capital. In this chapter we consider:

- the types of finance that are suitable for small businesses and the appropriate sources

- the criteria that potential investors in your business will use to evaluate your business

- the need for a carefully prepared business plan

A business must be adequately capitalized to survive. As we have seen from the earlier chapters, 'adequate' capitalization is a relative concept and depends on the optimum amounts of fixed and working capital required to generate a certain level of sales turnover. The tightly controlled business will require less capital than this optimum; the uncontrolled one will require a great deal more. Having assessed financial needs through the forecasting and budgeting activities discussed earlier and reviewed financial controls and ways of tightening up in such areas as stock and debtors, where the major share of working capital lies, our aim in this chapter is to investigate sources of external finance, their criteria for investing in small businesses and the best way to approach them.

Types and sources of finance

There are numerous *sources* of finance for small businesses, but very few *types* of finance are available. To work out which source to approach, the type of finance must first be determined by considering how much is required (the amount) in relation to how much the business already has of its own (the gearing), the use to which the finance will be put (the purpose), and for how long the finance will be required (the term). In considering whether you are likely to succeed in raising the finance, it is well worth asking why the source you choose to approach would want to give it to you. If *you* cannot find a reason, should they?

Since the first piece of information required is the amount, a cash flow forecast or projected balance sheet has to be prepared. Cash flow forecasts are more reliable for short periods, however, and being less technical are far easier to prepare. The question is: what type of finance should be entered into 'cash in'?

Equity

Equity is the name for money invested in the share capital of a company (or in the capital of a partnership or sole trader, although the term is normally reserved for companies alone) which is not to be repaid. The investment can be owned by anyone, whether they are full-time owners and employees of the business or external investors. The owners invest their own money in order to capitalize the business to begin trading (their prime motivation is to create a job for themselves or build a capital sum); outside investors (normally in the minority) invest on the basis that the business will grow and provide dividends and/or capital growth.

Equity investment is normally at risk. If the investment is in the form of *ordinary shares*, the shareholders are at the back of the queue in the event of the company's ceasing to trade; in the case of *preference shares*, the investors are preferred creditors if the company is wound up and rank behind other secured creditors and the Inland Revenue. Although ordinary shares carry a high degree of risk (the investor could lose the entire investment), they entitle the investor to dividends *if* they are declared. The shares can be sold at a capital gain, but only if a buyer can be found. Shares in small companies are difficult to sell since there is no ready market, and this tends to make them unattractive as an investment proposition. Preference shares, however, although less risky, entitle the investor to a 'coupon' or agreed rate of interest. There are various types of preference shares, each with their own advantages. They may also be sold, but the same disability applies – there is no ready market. Because of this lack of marketability, investors are likely to decide to invest either because they like you or because you have presented a very good case to indicate that the business has significant growth potential.

It follows from this that the most likely sources are the following:

(1) The present owners (in the form of a capital injection from savings or by retaining profits in the business).

(2) Family and friends, particularly those who are emotionally tied to you and can afford to risk losing their stake.

(3) Other private individuals who would like to be associated with a potentially exciting business venture, even if this does mean losing their stake. Finding private individuals with this risk profile will depend primarily on your social acquaintances, although there are other ways of identifying individual investors. Your accountant and other professional advisers will have clients who might consider such an investment. There are several publications which are geared specifically to private and institutional investment in small companies. They can be found in a good business library and are also advertised in the small business pages of the national press. Advertising for investors in the press is another option, although, because it is often seen as an exercise in desperation, it is likely to be considered last.

The incentive for individuals to invest in small companies has been greatly enhanced by the granting of tax relief for such investments under the Business Expansion Scheme. The Scheme allows private individuals subscribing for new shares in unquoted companies to offset their investment (a maximum of £40000 per annum) against taxable income at their highest marginal rate. What this means is that in effect the Inland Revenue pays for a large slice of the investment by crediting the investor's tax bill with the amount invested. There are several restrictions to the Scheme: for example investors may not be paid in their role as directors or managers and they must leave the investment in the company for at least five years. Notwithstanding these limitations, the Scheme is a considerable boost to private investment in small firms. Your accountant should be able to advise you on its suitability for your situation.

(4) Specialist financial institutions can be approached. The venture capital industry thrives on investments in smaller companies,

although most of these are in well-established, already profitable and not so small companies. There are a few venture capital investors who will consider amounts below £100000 but even these are difficult to find now. Venture capital is provided by some of the banks (which have specialist sections looking after equity investments) and a large number of independent and semi-independent institutions competing keenly in a small pool. Their names, addresses and investment criteria can be obtained from any one of a number of venture capital directories to be found in a good business or local reference library.

Venture capital has grown rapidly in recent years, buoyed up by tax incentives and a growing interest in the activities of small dynamic companies which could grow into the giants of tomorrow. The emergence of rapidly growing companies like Apple in the USA has spawned a new industry, dedicated to backing new ventures with substantial growth potential. Venture capital providers operate in the main on a portfolio basis, whereby they expect to lose some of their investments but have these more than covered by the 'winners'. If you are thinking of approaching one of these companies, therefore, you must generally have a proposition that excites and has the potential to grow into a medium-sized company within five years. The reason for this is that the investor is looking to generate substantial capital gain in as short a time as possible.

There are essentially two types of venture capital investors (although several variations exist within these categories): *hands-on*, whereby they require a seat on the board and will want a role in strategy formulation and key decision making, and *hands-off*, whereby the investor leaves the management of the company entirely to the managers. These investors normally want a minority stake in the company and are prepared to offer a package of equity and loans. You are advised to consult an accountant if you think that your business proposition requires venture capital, because you will need a business plan of some considerable complexity and assistance in negotiating a favourable deal – if you have to sell some of the equity, you will want to get the maximum in return.

(5) For the medium-sized company, the *Third Market* and *Unlisted Securities Market* (USM) provide alternative financing options. Raising new capital through a launch on either of these markets is

appealing to a company looking for more substantial sums (typically over £500000) and the glamour that accompanies a flotation. The USM can help companies with pre-tax profits in excess of £500000, whereas the Third Market offers more scope for smaller companies, including the more ambitious company which has recently started. The main advantages of a listing on either of these markets are as follows: the costs are considerably lower than a full listing on the Stock Exchange; the listing and reporting requirements are far less onerous than a full listing; a minimum of only 10 per cent (USM) of the equity need be sold (the minimum for a full listing is 25 per cent).

The so-called *Over-The-Counter* (OTC) market exists to provide finance for companies not seeking a formal listing on any market. The OTC market lies outside the Stock Exchange's control. Several 'market makers' operate in the OTC, matching buyers with sellers on a regular or *ad hoc* basis.

Debt finance

Debt or loan finance is money lent by an individual or institution which will be repaid over an agreed period, with interest paid by the borrower on any amounts outstanding. The lender is concerned to make sure that the money is repaid in full, making profit on the interest. The main sources of debt finance are the banks, comprising the big five high street names and a large number of smaller ones, although there is no reason why private individuals should not lend money to a business. In many smaller companies the directors themselves provide loans to the business, preferring to finance it this way rather than with equity, for the reason that directors' loans can be withdrawn readily without any tax complications. (Share capital cannot be withdrawn easily.)

The borrower should prepare a detailed business plan with cash flow forecasts before approaching a bank. (We cover such a business plan a little later.) Other than consulting the plan and taking a view on the viability of the business, before deciding to lend the following factors will be taken into consideration by the lender.

1 The purpose for which the funds are required: we have seen that there are principally two types of investment: fixed capital and

working capital. In the case of the former, the borrower should specify the type of equipment, vehicle or building being purchased, its expected useful life and resale value, and why it is needed in the business.

2 The amount relative to the equity in the business: there are two reasons why this is important. The lender will feel that, without owner's equity, he or she could easily walk away if things went awry, leaving the lender to try to salve something from the wreckage. Of equal importance is the question of servicing the debt. Highly geared companies (where loan capital is a high proportion of the total) are at greater risk because of the burden of having to service the debt.

3 The ability of the business to meet interest and capital repayments: the lender will want to see detailed and accurate cash flow forecasts for a two year period and profit forecasts for possibly up to five years, as evidence that the business has built repayments into its budgets and is not being adversely affected thereby.

4 The available security to cover the outstanding monies owed in the event of the business ceasing to trade. Security can take two main forms: business assets which have a market value, including fixed assets, stock and debtors, and personal assets, such as a house, shares and jewellery. The question of taking personal security raises the temperature of most business owners and at times the bank's attitude seems quite unreasonable. However, in the light of the risks involved, the failure rates of small businesses, the fact that privately owned firms are notoriously difficult to keep under surveillance and the often pitifully small amounts of personal finance committed to the business by the owners, asking for personal security seems quite justifiable.

Loans may be made on a secured or unsecured basis, depending on the amount borrowed and the status of the borrower. The bank might lend on an unsecured basis if only a small amount is required and the borrower can be trusted to repay the loan. Security is normally required for larger amounts (there is no absolute figure) irrespective of the standing of the borrower. Security on business assets can be in the form of a *floating charge*, whereby the charge 'floats' over all the assets in the business (fixed as well as current assets), or a *fixed charge*, which attaches to a particular asset or assets, usually the asset being purchased with the loan. The charges are registered at the Land Registry and the business cannot dispose of the assets charged without the bank's permission. The effect of securing the loan on an asset is to reduce the risk to the bank and therefore the interest payable by the borrower.

An alternative form of security is the provision of a personal or third party guarantee. The proprietors of unincorporated businesses are automatically at risk (they have unlimited liability), but directors of limited companies are not and would normally be asked to provide personal guarantees for smaller loans or overdrafts. A third party guarantee could be equally effective, although it is more difficult to find another party to provide the guarantee. This could be a family member (as an alternative to lending money), and certain local authorities are prepared to provide loan guarantees for companies offering benefits to the local area (such as jobs for local residents).

In the event of there being insufficient or no personal security available, the borrower can request that the loan be made under the government-backed Loan Guarantee Scheme. The scheme provides for a government guarantee of 70 per cent of the loan which is made in the normal way by a bank. The guarantee is invoked only if the business cannot repay the loan to the bank. Businesses may borrow up to £75000 under the Scheme (there is an effective lower limit of around £10000), and the eligibility criteria include the inability of the borrower to provide personal security. The government charges an interest premium of 2.4 per cent, which is payable quarterly, on top of the bank's variable interest rate. Repayment over a period of two to seven years is permitted and a capital moratorium (a holiday on capital repayments) can be provided in the first two years. The total interest payable is normally slightly above the rate charged by the banks for a secured loan.

The terms of repayment of bank loans can be negotiated to suit the cash flow of the business, and banks have a large number of special packages to suit different situations. Loans are divided into short-term lines of credit and term loans over a longer period.

The *overdraft* is used to cover fluctuations in the bank balance typically as a result of having to pay out money before cash from sales materializes. The overdraft is a short-term line of credit and is normally negotiated for a maximum of 12 months, but can also be arranged for a shorter, more specific period. The major advantage of an overdraft is that the business incurs interest payments only when overdrawn (whereas a term loan incurs interest payments whatever the bank balance). The rate of interest charged for a secured or unsecured overdraft will vary according to the amount and the standing of the borrower. About 3 per cent (secured) to 5 per cent (unsecured) over the base rate are typical overdraft rates for small businesses. Once the overdraft facility has been agreed with the bank, a facility letter to the borrower should follow setting out the period of the facility, the rate of interest charged and any other conditions.

A *term loan* is a fixed amount for an agreed period of time with a fixed or variable repayment schedule, payable either monthly or quarterly. A term loan is used to finance specific requirements, e.g. the purchase of equipment. The period is normally from two to seven years, although longer terms are available for specific purposes, such as the financing of buildings through commercial mortgages. The rule of thumb is that the term of the loan should match the useful life of the asset being purchased. The borrower would normally have a choice between fixed and variable interest rates: the former are fixed for the period of the loan and, depending on the outlook for interest rates, could be either above or below prevailing market rates; the latter vary as the base rate varies. Fixed rates are more advantageous in periods of high and rising interest rates, whereas they are a disadvantage when interest rates are on a downward spiral. One other advantage of the former is that the rate, being fixed, ensures regular and equal repayments which can more easily be planned into cash flow forecasts.

Choosing a bank

The growing complexity of the financial marketplace necessitates choosing the right bank. A bank manager with whom you can work and who understands your business is a major asset. Finding this person takes time. The starting point is 'which bank?' The major clearing banks offer a wide range of services and are probably best placed to serve the needs of most businesses. The smaller banks might lend on more risky propositions (this is one of the ways they would compete) but on less favourable terms. Most banks are competing keenly for new business accounts and the well-organized and well-prepared small business owner is in a good position to negotiate a favourable deal.

When opening a new account (or moving your present one) it is worth 'shopping around' to establish what is on offer, and there is scope to negotiate bank charges (many banks are prepared to offer free banking in the first year) and interest rates (if you can offer security or a personal guarantee there are significant gains to be made). Even the question of security could be negotiable: by approaching a bank with a well-written business plan and a satisfactory trading history, you could persuade the bank manager to accept a personal guarantee only. The interest rate payable on the overdraft facility should also be negotiable once you have established a history of profit and a stable relationship with the bank.

Choosing a particular branch will depend on what the business does and where it is located. There are three criteria for making a choice. A high street branch will understandably have many personal and retailing accounts, whereas one in or close to an industrial area will have a balance of personal and manufacturing accounts. Thus the potential customer should attempt to find out what type of commercial accounts bank at the branch in question. A particular branch could acquire a reputation for dealing with certain kinds of business activity and the accumulated expertise there could suit your business. The size of the branch is another criterion of choice. Small branches generally have one or two managers who may not have the discretionary lending levels that you require. This is likely to result in delays when you need a quick lending decision. Thus if the business is very small and unlikely to require more than a small overdraft from time to time, a small local branch might be adequate. For the larger account where there are more specialist needs, a larger branch is to be recommended where there will certainly be an appropriate degree of expertise. Finding the right size of branch is simply a matter of asking the right questions.

The final criterion is the experience and personality of the individual banker. Because inter-personal factors are the final determinant of a satisfactory banking relationship, your choice will be affected by how well you get on at a personal level. So when interviewing bank managers, you should evaluate their interest in your business and in you and their willingness to put some time into developing a relationship. Banking relationships are built on reciprocity and you should be clear about the effort that you are prepared to put into building a relationship with the bank manager. This does not necessarily mean inviting him or her to lunch every week, but rather how well you keep the bank informed about progress and prospects. Regular reports or telephone calls to the bank (say every quarter) will pay dividends when you suddenly need urgent financial assistance to take advantage of a major opportunity.

Asset finance

Asset finance, such as hire purchase or lease purchase, is used to fund the purchase of specific assets which essentially remain the lender's property until the debt is repaid. Generally the interest rate is higher and the repayment terms less negotiable than with a bank loan, but the major benefit of asset finance is that repayments are spread over the borrowing term. An additional and very important benefit is that, because asset finance comes from a separate source, spreading your borrowing as a matter of financial policy also reduces the risk associated with being dependent on one source of finance. Lenders are interested in knowing that if the business defaults, they can get their money back by repossessing the asset. Most of the banks have their own finance companies specializing in this type of finance. There are many independent finance houses also.

Lending decisions are based on the following:

1 the proportion of the total value of the asset to be financed, since in certain cases the lender requires that the borrower puts down a deposit of a proportion of the purchase price;
2 the second-hand value of the asset which, if the lender were to repossess it, could be re-sold to another buyer;
3 the useful life of the asset, which determines the repayment period and the residual value of the asset at the end of the agreement.

The best known example of asset finance is *hire purchase*. The buyer puts down a deposit amounting to upwards of 10 per cent of the purchase price and the balance plus interest incurred is paid off over an agreed period on a monthly repayment basis. Hire purchase is a realistic form of finance for new businesses as the lender has the comfort of the borrower putting down a deposit. Ownership does not pass to the buyer until the last payment has been made, although the value of the asset increases in the balance sheet as the repayments accumulate. Hire-purchase payments do not attract VAT.

Leasing (financial leasing) is similar to hire purchase in that the asset is financed over an agreed period. In this case, a small deposit is paid (typically three months' rental) and the asset is in effect rented to the borrower who pays a monthly or quarterly charge. Lease payments attract VAT at the standard rate. New businesses find it difficult to lease assets because leasing companies normally require three years' accounts as evidence of financial stability.

Contract rental of motor vehicles is an alternative form of asset finance, whereby the vehicle is rented to the buyer for an agreed period. The buyer has to state a maximum mileage for the period on which the rental payments are calculated. This can be an advantageous way to acquire the use of a vehicle at lower cost, particularly as all servicing and repairs are the responsibility of the renter. Contract rental also attracts VAT.

Factoring has grown in recent years as an important source of finance for working capital. A factoring company manages your sales ledger, advancing up to 80 per cent of monthly invoiced sales. The advantage to you is that there are almost no debtors to be financed, since the factor looks after the collection of debts. The costs of factoring vary: the factoring company charges interest on the advance, normally at the prevailing overdraft rate, and a commission based on sales income for managing the sales ledger. Factoring will suit only certain types of businesses.

Invoice discounting is a related service whereby sales invoices are sold at a discount to a discount house. The main difference between factoring and invoice discounting is that the latter does not involve managing the sales ledger.

Export finance is a specialized form of finance which we shall not deal with here. Exporters should consult their bank or other specialist advisers.

Supplier credit

Supplier credit is an important source of short-term finance. It is customary for suppliers to grant credit to customers and we saw earlier that it is up to the latter to negotiate the most favourable credit terms. The length of credit given and the willingness to give credit will depend upon the industry. Suppliers of *goods* often only give credit to allow accounts departments time to process invoices, and without trade references it can be difficult for a new business to obtain immediate credit. In this case, paying cash on delivery would be normal for a few months until you establish your credibility. Suppliers of *equipment* may sometimes agree to stage payments or hire purchase as they would have the right to recover the equipment under certain conditions (such as non-payment).

Grants

Grants from public or voluntary sector sources are normally not repayable, do not attract interest payments and thus constitute the cheapest form of finance. Consequently they are not easy to obtain. Grant-making authorities are likely to apply special criteria and the amounts available are likely to be limited both absolutely and in proportion to the overall capital of the business. In general, it may be necessary to show that the business is unable to raise the necessary finance from other sources. There are numerous grant-making authorities in the UK and directories of grants and other forms of financial assistance can be consulted in a business or reference library. The major sources are borough councils and local enterprise agencies (mainly rent, premises and start-up grants, particularly if they operate an ethnic minority or cooperatives policy), special bodies such as the Prince's Youth Business Trust (for people below the age of 26) and the Crafts Council who make grants to certain categories of business, and government departments (such as the Training Agency through which the Enterprise Allowance Scheme is available).

Criteria for investment in small businesses

Before writing a business plan for presentation to a bank or venture capital investor, the writer should have a clear idea of the criteria used to evaluate the business idea. These criteria are largely unwritten and any one banker will probably place more emphasis on some rather than others. Nevertheless, they will help in developing a convincing case, complete with all the necessary evidence that a banker requires.

The product

There is a logical sequence to an enquiry about any business and its activities, starting with the questions 'what does/will it sell?' and 'what is so special or different about the product or service?' The latter is called the *unique selling point* (USP), and simply describes the main product features and benefits that will make it stand out from the competition. This informs the banker that the business will be trying to *differentiate* its products from the competition and that a higher than otherwise gross profit margin can be sustained. Other than the USP, the product's *readiness for market* and likely *development costs* will be of concern, for the reason that products with indeterminate development programmes are too risky for most financial institutions. A very few might be interested if exceptionally high profitability can be demonstrated. (In other words, they might back the project on the grounds that, if it succeeds, they will make exceptional gains.) However, remember that your local bank is *not* a venture capital provider. You will have to approach the specialists described earlier.

The market

There are three critical issues concerning the market which an investor will want answered. The *growth and maturity* of the market is the first. The higher the growth rate, the more scope there is for making mistakes and the less severe the market is on inexperienced operators. The newer the market, the more the business will have to spend on educating it to use the product. The second issue concerns the *behaviour of customers* and their price sensitivity. People's buying habits (which are extraordinarily difficult to change) give a vital clue to their propensity to consider buying a new product; if they are to be persuaded to shift their loyalties, it is desirable that price is not the major incentive. Evidence to this effect would suggest that gross profit margins would not be under pressure, even if competitors were to make their presence felt. The third and final issue is one of *evidence of demand.* The best evidence is having made a sale, convinced a prospect to place an order or persuaded a prospect to confirm their intention to do so. If there are difficulties with all these issues (and yet you are convinced that a market exists), we are once again talking about high risk venture capital and the choice of financial institutions narrows quite appreciably.

Production

The financial and marketing implications of the *make or buy* decision could be decisive. If the strengths of the business are in marketing, then putting the work out to subcontractors should be seriously considered; however, if production is a strength, perhaps marketing should be bought in. Of concern too is the nature of the *technology* used in the production process and whether there could be technical problems delaying the launch of the product; the *sourcing* of materials, particularly if the business is dependent on key suppliers, should be covered satisfactorily.

Management

The *experience and knowledge of the management team* (or of the individual owner) should head the list of criteria since the ability to organize and manage the production, marketing, personnel and financial functions is arguably the *sine qua non* of all business success. *Personal qualities* of managers including commitment, motivation and values are also of prime importance, because backing small businesses is really all about backing people.

Finance

A successful business must have *adequate capital* if it is to survive the vagaries of the marketplace. In order to achieve adequacy, the effects of *gearing* (the relationship of the owner's stake to the amount sought) will be taken into account. The financial forecasts must be *realistic* and the *deal* offered (the proportion of equity offered to the amount of finance sought) must be attractive.

The business plan

The above five criteria must 'stack up' in a well-organized, well-argued and well-presented business plan. Details of this plan are discussed below. When using the plan to raise finance, remember that financiers frequently receive plans like yours. To stand out from the crowd, the plan must be different and have some obvious attraction for the reader. It must be sent in advance of any meeting and should preferably be expected – in other words, you should make contact with the banker or financier so that they know that you will be sending the plan.

The business plan

A business plan is a written document setting out the business idea in concise detail. It must demonstrate at least two things: first, that the business will generate a profit; second, that you (and your management team, if you have one) have the qualities to make it work. The plan is never complete – in a constantly changing world, it should be regarded as a living document requiring periodic updating.

It is used first and foremost as a means of communicating the nuts and bolts of the business idea to interested parties, although this is not its only purpose. Above all, as a written statement it has certain limitations and therefore should ideally be used as a preliminary communication to be followed up by spoken contact. This will not always be possible, however, and in some cases the plan must stand on its own as a complete and authoritative document.

The purpose

There are four essential reasons for writing a business plan:

1 to provide information about the business and the intentions of the owners, for whatever purpose;
2 to convince a third party to provide the necessary resources or to influence people who might be in a position to provide assistance of some form;

3 to develop the strategic thinking and tactical plans of the owners and in particular to demonstrate how the different parts of the business fit together in a coherent and profitable whole;

4 to set financial targets and detailed budgets against which the actual costs and revenues can be monitored and controlled.

The recipient

Before writing the plan, consider who it is aimed at, because individual readers will have different reasons for reading it (therefore they will expect to see different things in it) and varying lengths of time available to read and digest it (therefore they will have different priorities). Plans are normally written for the following people.

The bank manager

You will be approaching the bank manager for an overdraft facility or term loan, which must be repaid out of profits. They are therefore interested in viability (when will the business move into profit?) and cash flow (how much money will be needed to fund the business?). This suggests that profit and cash forecasts are required. However, since no one can accurately predict the future, they are also likely to want to know what business or personal assets are available as security, although it is not generally advisable (for psychological reasons) to put this information into the written plan.

Other financial backers

There are various kinds of investors whom you might have to influence:

1 *private individuals*, including partners, who will want to know how much risk they are taking, what role they are being asked to play in the business and how and when they will be able to get their money out;

2 *specialist financial institutions*, including venture capital investors, who will want the same information as private individuals but will be more interested in the balance between risk and return,

particularly in the prospect of a large capital gain (although some venture capital backers are also interested in short-term income).

Public authorities

Central and local government authorities and public sector institutions will be interested in the same factors as private financial backers, but additionally they will wish to know what private sector involvement is forthcoming (some public authorities will only assist if no private backing can be raised) and what wider social and economic benefits will result from the investment (the creation of jobs has become increasingly important).

Professional advisers

Your accountant, solicitor and other advisers will need to know what your plans are if they are to stay close to you and help you over the hurdles that lie ahead.

You and your management team

However tempting it may be to produce figures just to convince a backer, you should also believe them yourself! The business plan is a mechanism for reducing risk by weighing up the uncertainties in the external environment and planning to reduce them. It also acts to bring the combined intellectual efforts of the management team to bear on the problems and opportunities that lie ahead and, in so doing, makes a small contribution to corporate culture and team building.

Landlords, customers and suppliers

You might wish to inform other influential people outside the business about your business plans, if this is in your interests.

Presentation

There are a few essential points to bear in mind when writing the plan:

1 The plan should be written by the owner or by the management. In so doing you will improve your understanding of the business and will consequently be in a position to justify your statements and forecasts. Make use of your accountant to help with the figures and staff to provide detail on the individual sections.
2 Write enough to meet the plan's specific purpose but no more. The body should be about 10 pages excluding appendices. The reader is likely to be reading many such plans and will consequently devote only a limited amount of time to it.
3 To keep the reader's attention, the plan must be interesting and readable. Use everyday language and avoid technical terminology; use appendices for technical and supplementary information (initially of only marginal interest to the non-technical reader).
4 Use headings as much as possible to divide up the text in order to provide clarity and readability. Type the plan and present a neat copy.
5 Justify your forecasts with as much evidence as you can provide (your own beliefs and opinions are not evidence). Forecasts should be realistic, neither too gloomy nor over-ambitious. Err on the side of caution rather than optimism.

The forecasting period

The plan must show that the business will generate a profit and sufficient cash in order to repay its creditors (at base) and also show an appropriate return on investment over time. How long this will take depends on individual circumstances, but as a general rule most plans should look ahead at least two years in detail and up to five in broad outline.

The contents

A checklist of points for inclusion follows. Do not use them all, rather selecting those which are appropriate to your case. An example of a short business plan is appended to this chapter.

1 *Front page*
Business name
Proposer's name
Date

2 *Contents page*

Outline of contents

3 *Summary*

Summarize the completed plan in four short paragraphs with the intention of convincing the reader that an exciting investment opportunity beckons.

main products and markets
reasons for success
total funding showing internal and external sources
amount sought and terms required

4 *History of the business*

Statement of business objectives
The business in relation to the rest of the industry
Short history of the business to date, covering

year started and why
legal structure
ownership details
products or services offered
production capabilities
major customers and customer groups
management, key personnel, employees
finance
Refer to five years' historical accounts appended

5 *Origin of the idea or new plans*

How the idea came about
What prompted the new plans

6 *Products and services*

Description of products/services by group
Costs, prices and margins
Unique or special characteristics (USP)
New products/services being launched
Product development in hand, development costs, time scale
Product development plans

7 *Markets and marketing*

Customer profile (by segment):

    names (if appropriate)
    numbers
    geographical location
    socio-economic characteristics (income, age, etc.)
    industry characteristics (retail, production, etc.)
    purchasing behaviour/preferences

Size of the total market (value and volume)
Market share
Trends in the market
Market research findings and test market results (if any)
Special relationships with customers, orders taken
Competition:

    names of major competitors
    products and marketing
    prices
    reaction of competitors to new plans

Pricing, discount structure, incentives
Distribution channels
Method of physical distribution and costs
Promotional and selling plans and costs
Marketing and sales strategy, launch arrangements
Sales forecasts:

    by product and market for five years
    monthly detail for next 12 months
    sales forecasts for old and new business
    justification for sales forecasts

8 *Production, purchasing and sources of supply*

Equipment, premises, production methods
New equipment requirements, prices, availability
New premises requirements, rents, availability
Staffing of production, key skills
Future staffing requirements, availability
Subcontractors and arrangements
Supply sources

9 *Management and human resources*

Organization structure
Owners' and managers' names and personal details
Ownership details
Qualifications, experience, skills
Staff numbers and categories of work
Future staffing requirements, availability
Training facilities

10 *Finance*

Summary of financial results and finance sought:
    sales and profit targets
    return on sales and on investment
    equity and/or loans required, terms, repayments
Audited accounts for five years
Sales forecasts for five years
Forecast annual profit and loss accounts for five years
Forecast annual balance sheets for five years
Monthly cash flow forecast for next 12 months
Key business ratios
Sensitivity analysis on best guess and pessimistic scenarios
Assumptions and major risks

11 *Appendices*

Product costings
Owners' and directors' CVs
Product drawings, photographs
Product technical details
Market research details
Confirmation of orders received or intentions to order
Equipment details
Premises details
Other details not presented earlier

Key points

- Equity capital, the most permanent in the business, normally comes from the owners, but there is now an important infrastructure of external equity available from private and institutional sources.
- For most small businesses, the bank is the main external source of finance and most larger banks have a wide range of lending services to suit every need.
- Because banks are not in the business of taking risks (it is up to the entrepreneur to do this), some form of security is nearly always required in the form of either business or personal assets.
- The government-backed Loan Guarantee Scheme can help where there are no business assets and the owner does not have sufficient personal security for the loan.
- The overdraft should be used only to finance short-term fluctuations in working capital; term loans over several years should be used to finance equipment, vehicles and buildings.
- It is now widely accepted that a Business Plan is a necessity when approaching a bank for finance and that it should be written by the borrower, not by the firm's professional advisers.

Appendix: Business plan for a sole trader, Wayne Lawrence t/a 'Jacket-in' at Kingston Business Centre, West London, September 1988

Contents

- The business idea
- The market
- Marketing
- Premises and equipment
- Suppliers
- Finance

- Costings
- Sales forecast year 1, year 2
- Cash flow forecast year 1, year 2
- Profit and loss account year 1, year 2
- Balance sheet year 1, year 2

The business Idea

I want to manufacture men's jackets from a small workshop in Kingston, to sell to retailers or wholesalers in the West London area. I have trained and worked as a machinist and pattern cutter for several years and recently I have been making clothes for friends and family in my spare time.

A friend has said he would order from me if I could start producing on a commercial basis, and from preliminary research I believe that other retailers would be interested. I have chosen to manufacture jackets because they allow a reasonable profit margin, the market is not too saturated and styles can be changed without major pattern changes simply by varying fabric colour, pocket shape, motifs etc. I have done two sets of costings for jackets, a quilted ski-type jacket and a lightweight summer jacket.

I shall be working alone initially as I have kept my sales target well within my own production capacity.

The market

I am aiming at the fashion-conscious 16–35 year old male as the end user of this product, although my main market will be small retailers or wholesalers wanting jackets made to their own specifications. There are many clothes businesses which do not want to order in large bulk, and prefer to order in dozens on a month by month basis. I will also be able to offer delivery within a week.

The clothing trade is very competitive but consumers are now looking for quality rather than cheapness, and I feel that too many manufacturers are still price sensitive, leaving a gap in the market for producers of quality goods. I have selected West London as my target area because there are many retailers in this area who feel compelled to travel into Central London or even the East End to visit suppliers as there are so few in West London.

Marketing

Most of my sales promotion will be through personal calls on prospects, because traders, whether retail or wholesale, like to see samples before they order. No one will order a new range from a brochure or pamphlet – unless they are very confident of your standards. Therefore a large part of my promotion budget is for transport expenses. I will try to coordinate delivery of an order with a sales appointment to save time and money.

I will place the business name and address in the Yellow Pages and Business Pages for the South West London district, but will not advertise in trade papers until I can be sure of meeting demand.

As I can offer an all-round personal service, i.e. producing to customer requirements, small batch size and delivery service, I feel that I will appeal to the trader who is conscious of the image of his/her business.

Premises and equipment

I intend to move into premises in the Kingston Business Centre, which is specially designed to accommodate small and growing businesses. There are small units available; the rent I have quoted in my cash flow is for a 200 sq.ft. workshop on the ground floor. The price is inclusive of rates, but three months rent is required in advance.

Although I have accumulated equipment relevant to the business, such as a sewing machine, shears, tapes, etc., I still require the following equipment.

	£	
Small van (second-hand)	2000	(depreciation over 2 yrs)
Overlocker	600	(depreciation over 3 yrs)
Industrial sewing machine	450	(depreciation over 3 yrs)
Work-table	120	
Dummy	80	
Tapes, scissors, pins	50	
Irons × 2	50	
Boards × 2	50	
Total cost	3400	

Suppliers

My main supplier will be Chameleon Fabrics Ltd, Lily Lane Trading Estate, Sutton, Surrey.

Although they supply large manufacturers they also sell to the public in small quantities. This means that I can not only buy my primary colour fabrics in bulk, but also buy small quantities of less popular colours as I need them. I have purchased from them on a small purchase basis for several months, and I have been advised that I will be offered credit facilities if I require them. (I shall probably opt for prompt payment discount rather than credit facilities.)

Finance

As the Premises and Equipment section shows, I require £3400 for equipment and £650 for advance rent payments. I require an overdraft limit of £4000, although my forecasts indicate that I may not require quite this amount. I have enclosed cash-flow forecasts and financial statements for the first two trading years, in order that a better picture of the business's financial situation may be gained. Assumptions in these forecasts are as follows (annotations relate to cash flows).

Year 1

1 See Sales Forecast.
2 See costings; July includes £380 of closing stock.
3 Drawings only; a moderate salary for myself.
4 See Premises and Equipment.

Year 2

1 Selling price increased by 5 per cent to account for inflation.
2 Purchase price increased by 5 per cent to account for inflation.
3 Drawings increased by 10 per cent.
4 Replacement iron, an additional dummy plus smaller pieces of equipment, e.g. shears.

Costings

Quilted jackets £

Batch size of 48		£
	Fabrics 48 × 1½m × £3	216
	Zips etc. 48 × various × 50p	24
	Quilting 48 × 1½m × £1.33	96
	Lining 48 × 1½m × 66p	48
	Total	384

Therefore Material cost of 48 jackets is £384 (excl. VAT)
Selling price of 48 jackets is £864 (excl. VAT)
Gross profit on 48 jackets is £480

Labour

Batch size of 48	Cutting out	2 hours
	Pinning/zips	8 hours
	Sewing up	12 hours
	Pressing	1 hour 40 mins
	Total	23 hours 40 mins

Therefore at least 24 hours *or* 3 days work per batch of 48 jackets

Lightweight Jackets £

Batch size of 48		£
	Fabric 48 × 1½m × £2	144
	Zips etc. 48 × various × 50p	24
	Lining 48 × 1½m × £1	72
	Total	240

Therefore Material cost of 48 jackets is £240 (excl. VAT)
Selling price of 48 jackets is £600 (excl. VAT)
Gross profit of 48 jackets is £360

Labour

Batch size of 48	Cutting out	2 hours
	Pinning/zips	4 hours
	Sewing up	8 hours
	Pressing	1 hour 40 mins
	Total	15 hours 40 mins

Therefore 16 hours *or* 2 days work per batch of 48 jackets

'Jacket-in' sales forecast. Business name: 'Jacket-in'. Year 1, year 2

	Aug	Sep	Oct	Nov	Dec	Jan	Feb	Mar	Apr	May	Jun	Jul	Total
Year 1													
Sales volume (dozens) quilted	8	16	12	16	16	8	4						76
Sales value (£)	1730	3460	2590	3460	3460	1730	870						16430
Sales volume (dozens) lightweight	2							8	10	12	12	10	54
Sales value (£)	300							1200	1500	1800	1800	1500	8100
Total sales value	2030	3460	2590	3460	3460	1730	870	1200	1500	1800	1800	1500	24530
Year 2													
Sales volume (dozens) quilted	10	20	20	18	18	10	8						104
Sales value (£)	2270	4540	4540	4080	4080	2270	1810						23590
Sales volume (dozens) lightweight	4						4	10	16	20	16	12	82
Sales value (£)	630						630	1580	2520	3150	2520	1890	12920
Total sales value	2900	4540	4540	4080	4080	2270	2440	1580	2520	3150	2520	1890	36510

Cash flow forecast. Business name: 'Jacket-in'. Year 1

Notes		Aug	Sep	Oct	Nov	Dec	Jan	Feb	Mar	Apr	May	Jun	Jul	Total
1	CASH IN													
	Sales	2030	3460	2590	3460	3460	1730	870	1200	1500	1800	1800	1500	25400
	Output VAT	300	520	390	520	520	260	130	180	230	270	270	230	3820
	Own funds	1000												1000
	Loans													
	E.A.S.	170	170	180	170	170	180	170	170	180	170	170	180	2080
	Total	3500	4150	3160	4150	4150	2170	1170	1550	1910	2240	2240	1910	32300
2	CASH OUT													
	Purchases/suppliers	890	1540	1150	1540	1540	770	380	480	600	720	720	980	11310
	Rent	650	220	220	220	220	220	220	220	220	220	220	220	3070
	Rates													
	Power			180			220			200			180	780
	Legal fees													
	Insurance	250												250
	Repairs/maintenance							60						60
	Promotion/advertising	400	40	60	40	30	30	30	50	30	50	50	50	860

Item	1	2	3	4	5	6	7	8	9	10	11	12	Total
Travel/motoring	180	80	80	80	80	80	80	80	80	80	80	80	1060
Entertaining/catering													
Telephone			120			140			140			150	550
Postage	10	10	10	20	10	10	10	10	10	10	10	10	130
Printing/stationery	200					50							250
3 Drawings/salaries+NIC	540	540	540	540	540	540	540	540	540	540	540	540	6480
Audit/accountancy												300	300
Leasing/HP/hire													
Bank charges													
Overdraft interest			180			30							210
Loan interest													
Loan repayments													
4 Machinery/equipment	3400												3400
Other													
Input VAT	760	250	190	250	250	130	70	90	110	130	130	180	2540
VAT to C+E				10			670			270			950
Total	7280	2680	2730	2690	2680	2220	2060	1470	1930	2020	1750	2690	32200
Cash flow	(3780)	1470	430	1460	1470	(50)	(890)	80	(20)	220	490	(780)	100
Cum cash flow	(3780)	(2310)	(1880)	(420)	1050	1006	110	190	170	390	880	100	

Cash flow forecast. Business name: 'Jacket-in'. Year 2

Notes		Aug	Sep	Oct	Nov	Dec	Jan	Feb	Mar	Apr	May	Jun	Jul	Total
1	**CASH IN**													
	Sales	2900	4540	4540	4080	4080	2270	2440	1580	2520	3150	2520	1890	36510
	Output VAT	430	680	680	610	610	340	370	240	380	470	380	280	5470
	Own funds													
	Loans													
	Other													
	Total	3330	5220	5220	4690	4690	2610	2810	1820	2900	3620	2900	2170	41980
2	**CASH OUT**													
	Purchases/suppliers	1500	2020	2020	1810	1810	1010	810	630	1010	1260	1010	760	15650
	Rent	230	230	230	230	230	230	230	230	230	230	230	230	2760
	Rates													
	Power			240			290			240			200	970
	Legal fees	300												300
	Insurance	150						60						210
	Repairs/maintenance													
	Promotion/advertising	100	60	60	50	40	40	60	60	60	60	50	50	690

	1	2	3	4	5	6	7	8	9	10	11	12	
Travel/motoring	250	100	100	100	100	100	100	100	100	100	100	100	1350
Entertaining/catering													
Telephone		130			150			150			160		590
Postage	10	10	10	30	10	10	10	10	10	10	10	10	140
Printing/stationery	240				60								300
3 Drawings/salaries+NIC	600	600	600	600	600	600	600	600	600	600	600	600	7200
Audit/accountancy												320	320
Leasing/HP/hire													
Bank charges	30			30			30			30			120
Overdraft interest	30												30
Loan interest													
Loan repayments													
4 Machinery/equipment						100							100
Other													
Input VAT	320	330	350	300	290	220	150	120	200	210	170	210	2870
VAT to C+E	330			790			750			520			2390
Total	4030	3350	3800	3890	3100	2840	2770	1750	2650	2990	2170	2650	35990
CASH FLOW	(700)	1870	1420	800	1590	(230)	40	70	270	630	730	(500)	
CUM CASH FLOW	(600)	1270	2690	3490	5080	4850	4890	4960	5230	5860	6590	6090	
£100 c. fwd.													

Profit and loss account

	Year 1		Year 2	
	£	£	£	£
Sales		25400		36510
Cost of sales	11310		15650	
Opening stock	–		380	
Closing stock	380		380	
	10930	10930	15650	15650
Gross profit		14470		20860
Enterprise Scheme		2080		
		16550		
Rent	3070		2760	
Power	780		970	
Insurance	250		300	
Repairs	60		210	
Promotion/advertising	860		690	
Travel/motoring	1060		1350	
Telephone	550		590	
Postage	130		140	
Printing/stationery	250		300	
Drawings	6480		7200	
Accountancy	300		320	
Bank charges	–		120	
O/d interest	210		30	
Depreciation	1350		1350	
	15350	15350	16330	16330
Net profit		1200		4530

Balance sheet year 1, year 2

Fixed assets

Van and equipment	3400		3500	
Less depreciation	1350	2050	2700	800

Current assets

Stock	380		380	
Debtors	–		–	
Cash	100		6090	
	480		6470	

Current liabilities

Creditors	–		–	
VAT owed	330		540	
Overdraft	–		–	
Net current assets		150		5930
Net assets		2200		6730

Financed by:

Owner's funds		1000		1000
Reserves from P&L		1200		5730
		2200		6730

Supplementary Reading

Getting started

Starting a Business by Richard Hargreaves (Heinemann, London).
  Probably still one of the best texts around, written by someone
  with substantial experience of helping small firms.
Choosing, Buying and Running a Successful Retail Business by R.
  Fuller (Phoenix Publishing, London). One of the few books
  devoted specifically to retailing written by someone with retailing
  experience.

All the banks and larger firms of accountants have a series of free
booklets on getting started and a large number of books are available
at most reference libraries and bookshops.

Strategy

Competitive Strategy by Michael Porter (Free Press, London).
  Although written for the large company manager, this text is
  important reading for anyone wishing to understand corporate
  strategy.
Corporate Strategy by Igor Ansoff (Sidgwick and Jackson, London).
  An alternative treatment of strategy, although also with the
  company executive in mind.

Finance and accounting

Financial Management for the Small Business by Colin Barrow
  (Kogan Page, London). Still one of the better texts on accounting
  and finance for the small business person.
An Insight into Management Accounts by John Sizer (Pelican,
  London). An in-depth look at information systems and controls
  for larger companies.

Risk Capital for Small Firms by Small Business Research Trust/
Barclays Bank (SBRT, London). A recent publication full of
useful explanations of financial jargon and sources of finance.

The Business Plan Workbook by Colin and Paul Barrow (Kogan
Page, London). A very comprehensive guide to writing a plan.

Marketing and selling

Marketing Management by Philip Kotler (Prentice Hall, London). A
basic text from the guru of marketing, written for large companies
but useful background reading.

The Royal Mail Direct Mail Handbook by Les Andrews (Exley,
London). Full of useful tips on practical marketing.

How to Win Customers by Heinz Goldman (Pan, London). A solid
and invaluable guide to selling.

Organization and people

Understanding Organisations by Charles Handy (Penguin, London).
For a basic understanding of how organizations work and what to
think about when trying to build one.

Managing People at Work by John Hunt (Pan, London). An insight
into effective human relations management.

What Do You Mean 'Communication'? by Nicki Stanton (Pan,
London). An approach to communication in business that puts
people first.

ACAS (Advisory, Conciliation and Arbitration Service) provides
several free booklets on aspects of hiring and firing people, and is
also a source of advice for small businesses.

General

Exporting: Getting your Business off the Ground by Brian Ogley (PCP/
Barclays Bank, London). A useful text on the mechanics of
exporting.

The Small Business Guide by Colin Barrow (BBC, London). A useful reference book about sources of information and advice.

Directory of Franchising by Franchise World Magazine (Franchise World, London). A reference book on types of franchises and how to evaluate them.

Small Business Production/Operations Management by Terry Hill (Macmillan, London). One of the few books on production management written by someone with experience in the field.

Company Law Handbook edited by Keith Walmsley (Butterworths, London). Updated annually, this is a useful text on company law.

Law for the Small Business by Patricia Clayton (Kogan Page, London). The most concise and informative text on law for small businesses.

Taxation: there are several texts (e.g. Croner's and Tolley's which are updated annually.

Sources of information

Other than choosing the right professional advisers, there are numerous sources of local information for small businesses. The main ones are as follows.

Local Enterprise Agencies: they give free advice to small businesses and can be located in your area through the town hall, from directory enquiries or by phoning Business in the Community in London (01-253 3716). They are also a source of further help and can put you in touch with specific kinds of assistance.

Economic Development Office: your local town hall will have a section devoted to helping business.

Small Firms Service: this is a government body responsible for giving information to small businesses on almost any subject. They are to be found all over the country. Telephone Freephone Enterprise.

Business courses for small businesses: there are courses for start-ups and established businesses in your local area, sponsored by the Training Agency. Many are free or provided at subsidized fees. Telephone your local Training Agency area office through directory enquiries.

Glossary

accounting period   The period over which the accounts are drawn up (normally a year).

accrual   The accounting principle determining that costs should be matched to revenues in the same period.

acid test   The ratio of stock and debtors to current liabilities; the ultimate test of a firm's ability to meet its immediate debts.

analysed cash book   A cash book (cf.) showing an analysis of receipts and payments.

asset finance   Finance raised to cover the purchase of specific assets, such as hire purchase or leasing.

assets   Amounts owned by or owing to the business and therefore in its favour.

balance sheet   The financial statement showing total assets and liabilities of the business, and hence its net worth (cf.), and the way the business is financed.

breakeven   The point at which income from sales exactly covers costs.

budget   A detailed breakdown of forecast sales revenues and costs for a future period, usually produced for control purposes, against which actual revenues and costs can be assessed.

budgetary control   Using monthly budgets to control expenditure and monitor sales performance.

business entity   The accounting principle which states that the business is separate from its owners and employees.

business expansion scheme   A government scheme allowing private individuals subscribing for new shares in unquoted companies to offset their investment against their taxable income.

capital allowances   The statutory amount which the government allows the business to write down annually against its taxable income to provide for the using up of fixed assets (in place of depreciation).

cash book   The book of account recording bankings and payments.

cash flow   The difference between cash banked and cash paid out of the bank account.

conservatism   In preparing the accounts, if there is any doubt about profit, it should be understated rather than overstated.

consistency   Accounts should be compiled in a consistent way so they can be compared over the years.

corporate plan   A written plan setting out the objectives for a period and the strategy for achieving them together with financial forecasts.

cost of sales   The materials, stock and production costs associated with a given level of sales (cf. variable costs).

costing   The process whereby actual or estimated costs of a job are calculated preparatory to setting a price.

creditors   The amount owing to suppliers.

current assets   Amounts owned by or owing to the business which have a life of less than 12 months.

current liabilities   Amounts owing to suppliers and others (such as VAT, PAYE) which have a life of less than 12 months.

current ratio   The ratio of current assets to current liabilities measuring the firm's ability to meet its short-term debts.

debtors   The amount owing by customers.

declining balance   A method used to depreciate an asset whereby a percentage rate of depreciation is applied to the net book value of the asset at the end of each year.

depreciation   The amount set aside in the accounts annually to account for the using-up of the fixed assets (cf.) over their useful life.

direct costs   The costs directly relating to a sale, project or business activity.

directors' loan   A loan by the directors to the business.

dividends   A distribution of net profit after taxation to shareholders.

double-entry   Transactions entered in one book of account give rise to entries in another.

drawings   The amount taken out of the unincorporated business by the proprietor.

dual aspect   Part of the balance sheet which says that every transaction in the business must have a balancing transaction.

equity   The permanent finance in the business invested by the shareholders entitling them to a share of the profits.

extrapolation   A method of forecasting by establishing percentage changes in a set of historical figures over a period of years and using them to produce a set of forecasts.

factoring   A method of financing debtors whereby the factoring company advances an agreed proportion of the monthly sales and (normally) manages the sales ledger.

financial accounting   The study of historical financial information about the actual performance of the business such as profit and loss accounts and balance sheets.

financial stability   The ability to met short-term and long-term debts from normal business profits.

fixed assets   Assets, such as equipment, machinery, tools, vehicles, buildings, licences, leases and patents, which have a life of more than 12 months and are used to generate profit for the business.

fixed capital   The capital required to finance the long-term activities of the business, principally investments in plant, equipment, machinery and buildings.

fixed costs   Costs that can change but do not vary directly in proportion to changes in sales or output.

floating charge   A legal charge over all the assets in the business at any point in time.

funds flow statement   The financial statement showing where finance has come from (the sources) and where it has been used (the applications) in the period.

gearing   The ratio of borrowed capital to total capital employed (including borrowed and shareholders capital).

going concern   Valuing the assets of the business on the basis that it will survive rather than close down.

gross profit   The amount left over after deducting cost of sales from sales revenue.

hire purchase   A method of acquiring the ownership of an asset by putting down a deposit and paying off the balance over a given period including the capital sum and interest on the amount outstanding.

historical cost   The accounts are prepared on the basis of what was paid for things rather than what they are worth now or what they would cost to replace.

indirect costs   The costs incurred in running a business which are not directly related to a particular sale, project or business activity.

intangible assets   Fixed assets which do not have a physical, tangible presence such as leases and licences.

invoice discounting   A method of financing debtors whereby a discount house buys the outstanding invoices at a discount.

leasing   A method of acquiring the use of an asset (without necessarily its ownership) by paying a rental charge to the owner (usually a leasing company).

liabilities   Amounts owed by the business to others.

management accounting   Accounting for day-to-day management needs, particularly information required for decision-making.

materiality   Amounts should be treated in such a way in the accounts only if they matter or are material to the outcomes.

money measurement   The accounting principle determining that only transactions measured in money terms should be included in the accounts.

net assets   Total assets less current liabilities.

net book value   The residual value of the assets in the balance sheet after depreciation.

net current assets   *see* working capital.

net worth   The book value of the company after all liabilities have been met, as represented in the balance sheet.

nominal ledger   A book of account showing total invoiced sales to customers and payments by them and total invoiced purchases by suppliers and payments by the business, to produce total debtors and total creditors at the end of each month.

operating costs   *see* fixed costs.

over-the-counter market   An informal market for small company shares.

overdraft   A short-term line of credit from the bank granted for a fixed period, normally up to 12 months.

overhead recovery rate   The charge-out rate which covers total overhead costs.

overheads   The costs associated with running the business regardless of the actual level of sales achieved.

petty cash book   The book of account recording cash expenditure on small items of purchases.

profit   Normally net profit before tax; the surplus of invoiced sales revenue over total costs in a period.

profit and loss account   The financial statement showing sales revenue and total costs of making those sales and thus net profit or loss for a period.

purchases day book   A book of account with a chronological listing of invoiced purchases in each month.

purchases ledger   A book of account with a listing of invoiced purchases by and amounts paid to each supplier.

realization   The accounting principle determining that sales income is taken into the accounts at the time of invoicing (and not when the sales are paid).

receivables   *see* debtors.

reducing balance   *see* declining balance.

reserves   The accumulated profit reinvested in the business after all distributions.

retained profit   *see* reserves.

revaluation reserve   An amount arising when assets (such as a building) are revalued at a figure above their historical cost.

sales day book   A book of account with a chronological listing of invoiced sales in each month.

sales ledger   A book of account with a listing of invoiced sales to, and amounts paid by, each customer.

sales revenue   Invoiced sales for a period (also income, turnover).

sensitivity analysis   A method of evaluating financial outcomes by changing key assumptions in the forecasting equation.

share capital   The amount invested by the shareholders in the permanent capital of the business, entitling them to a share of the profits in the form of dividends.

share premium   The excess of the amount paid for a share above its par (original) value.

sources and applications of funds statement   *see* funds flow statement.

straight line   A method used to depreciate an asset whereby a fixed and equal amount is applied to the asset each year until its value is reduced to zero.

strategy   A game plan or overall coordinated approach to competing effectively and achieving long-term objectives.

SWOT   An analytical management tool standing for strengths, weaknesses, opportunities and threats.

tangible assets Fixed assets which have a physical, tangible presence, such as equipment, vehicles and buildings.

third market A market for the shares in smaller companies traded under greatly relaxed stock exchange regulations.

unlisted securities market A market for the shares in smaller companies traded under stock exchange regulations which are less rigid than those for a full listing.

variable costs Costs that vary directly in proportion to a change in sales or output.

variance analysis Establishing variances between budget and actual expenditure on a monthly basis and explaining the differences (cf. budgetary control).

venture capital Capital put at risk by the investor.

viability Generally any point at or beyond the breakeven (cf.)

work-in-progress The value put on work for customers which is yet to be invoiced.

working capital The capital required to finance the short-term activities of the business, principally the investment in stock and debtors.